T0246259

PRAISE FOR

Late Wonders

"Wesley McNair asks disarmingly in this abundant retrospective, 'Would it matter if I told you people live here?' Because it matters—and we matter—to McNair, he has become our great poet of American tenderness and loneliness. Amidst our general silence on the wounding of class, McNair has made that wounding—his own and others'—his theme, and so given us back an America we have all but thrown away. He has done this from a 'stubborn allegiance to the heart,' with deep love and respect for our common story as it is and not as it's falsified in advertising, politics, and popular culture. Early and late, Wesley McNair's democratic and generous body of work is a wonder."

—THOMAS R. SMITH, author of *Storm Island* and *Medicine Year*

"Wesley McNair writes that early in his life as a poet he 'already sensed the importance America would have in my future work.' Indeed, the America he so thoroughly imagines and generously shares in these striking and compassionate poems is both surprisingly familiar and unlike any to be found anywhere else in American poetry. It's a rural America that's often hidden from view, but in McNair's story we find the America we all live in, one fashioned out of endless striving, sorrow, and love for what's best and most lasting in our intimate and collective selves. Yes, finally, it's a love story, as new and ancient as our capacity to wonder, and praise."

—PHILIP SCHULTZ, author of *The Wherewithal*

ALSO BY WESLEY MCNAIR

POETRY
The Faces of Americans in 1853
The Town of No
My Brother Running
Talking in the Dark
Fire
The Ghosts of You and Me
Lovers of the Lost
The Lost Child
The Unfastening
Dwellers in the House of the Lord

LIMITED EDITIONS
Twelve Journeys in Maine
The Dissonant Heart
My Life in Cars

NONFICTION
Mapping the Heart: Reflections on Place and Poetry
The Words I Chose: A Memoir of Family and Poetry

Late Wonders

Late Wonders

NEW AND SELECTED POEMS

❧

Wesley McNair

BOSTON
GODINE
2022

Published in 2022 by
GODINE
Boston, Massachusetts

LIBRARY OF CONGRESS CATALOGING-IN-PUBLICATION DATA
Names: McNair, Wesley, author.
Title: Late wonders : new & selected poems / Wesley McNair.
Description: Boston : Godine, 2022.
Identifiers: LCCN 2022005061 (print) | LCCN 2022005062 (ebook) |
     ISBN 9781567927429 (hardback) | ISBN 9781567927436 (ebook)
Subjects: LCGFT: Poetry.
Classification: LCC PS3563.C388 L38 2022 (print) | LCC PS3563.C388
     (ebook) | DDC 811/.54--dc23
LC record available at https://lccn.loc.gov/2022005061
LC ebook record available at https://lccn.loc.gov/2022005062

First Printing, 2022
Printed in the United States of America

For my family

CONTENTS

WHERE I WOKE UP
A Retrospective

THE BOOK YOU HOLD in your hands contains writing I have done for fifty years as a poet, one poem lighting the way to the next and the next. By hindsight, it seems unlikely that such a tenuous process could have led to a book of selected poems at all. Yet as I wrote, slowly at first, then gaining speed, I was inspired by a growing vision of family, region, and nation, and the urgency of that vision carried me on. I begin with this foreword to tell you the story of how I came to create the poems I've assembled here.

In the years after I graduated from college, I found writing poetry nearly impossible. Marrying my wife Diane at the age of twenty-one, I inherited two children, whom I then adopted; later on, she gave birth to two more and ours became a family of six. Fatherhood, high-school teaching, and extra work during summers left me with little more than good intentions and unfinished drafts.

Still, I felt a deep need to make poems, which sometimes left me sick at heart. So, I looked up graduate schools that offered courses in writing poetry, discovering that one of them, the University of Iowa, not only granted degrees for poets but provided financial support for teaching assistants. Sending for an application, I fantasized about writing poems for a thesis while our family stayed in quarters reserved for graduate students. But when I received the paperwork and realized that an assistantship at Iowa could never support a family the size of mine even with scholarship aid, I didn't apply. It became apparent that if I wanted to become a poet, I'd have to stay put in rural New Hampshire and figure a way to do it by myself.

My first step was to set in motion a long-term plan to escape my crushing workload as a high-school teacher and make more room for poetry. I began attending the Bread Loaf School of English for part of each summer to obtain a master's degree, and in 1967, landed a position in the English department at Colby-Sawyer College, not far from my home. To strengthen my academic credentials, I then enrolled in Bread Loaf's advanced master's program. In the meantime, I gradually learned how to find holes in my busy schedule so I could read poems, memorize the ones I loved, and write lines, draft by draft, that matched the thoughts and music I carried in my head.

In today's MFA America, where people routinely learn how to write poems in poetry workshops taken for college credit, this may seem an unusual approach. Yet two or three generations ago, all poets were self-taught, guided by work they loved or readers they showed their poems to, and they would have thought it strange to become writers by earning grades in a classroom. Often, as in my case, they wrote first about the locations where they lived, which was their means of finding their place in the world. Many, like me, returned to explore those original places throughout their lives as poets.

As a developing writer, I was particularly drawn to my rural neighbors in New Hampshire. They may have seemed unremarkable, but having observed the people around me since boyhood, I understood they were as complicated and unusual as anyone else, and I itched to explore their complexities.

It's no accident, then, that country people appear often in my first two books. In fact, the final poem of my first collection, *The Faces of Americans in 1853*, affirms my bond with them. But when I worked on that book, I was also enthusiastic about American studies, founding a baccalaureate program at Colby-Sawyer College to study the cultural meanings of America. As a result, my first book includes satiric poems about popular culture, and poems about painters of the nineteenth century like the New England muralist Rufus Porter, who were influenced by American dreams and visions. The Porter poem and others in the collection suggest that I already sensed the importance America would have in my future work.

My second collection, *The Town of No* is more focused in its presentation of rural life. Its view of cultural change and dislocation in New England reflects a place I knew by heart. I spent my early childhood in Vermont, arriving in New Hampshire in 1953, when my stepfather moved the family there. As a teenager, I worked on large dairy farms along the Connecticut River, among the last still left. One summer, I lived with and worked alongside a Danish immigrant family who struggled with falling milk prices, barely able to break even. By the 1960s, that big farm and all the others in the state had disappeared, giving way to small parcels of land like my stepfather's, or house lots on new streets. Beginning with fragmentary memories from the agrarian past, *The Town of No* moves to poems about farmers losing their farms, family and community dysfunction, failed dreamers and sufferers, and people carrying on. As I wrote them, I learned how a book of poetry could evoke a cultural moment.

I also learned a way of working as a poet, using a common language and matter-of-fact approach to tease out a poem's feeling and take me inside the struggles and longings of those I wrote about.

My first reader and often my only one as I worked was Diane. Over the years, her creative interests have included ceramics, watercolors, and jazz vocals in performance, and she has always had an unusually intuitive understanding of poetry. But increasingly I turned also to Donald Hall. I was introduced to him by two former high-school students in 1975, shortly after he moved into his grandfather's farmhouse in Wilmot, just ten miles away from my own farmhouse. At the end of our first visit, I put a manuscript of my poems on his kitchen table, which he liked so much that it became the basis of an exchange of poems and letters between the two of us that lasted for the rest of his life. Don's unwavering belief in my poems in those early days was crucial to my growth as a poet. What's more, he procured a publisher for *The Town of No* and for every collection I wrote afterward, including this one. In the fall of 1985, unbeknown to me, Don invited David Godine to his house, where he proposed that David publish my second book. David agreed, and Godine has been my publisher ever since.

In 1987, I left New Hampshire to take a position as a poet at the University of Maine at Farmington. In west Central Maine, I found a New England unlike the one I'd left behind—its towns less groomed, its back roads unpredictable and mysterious. Settling in the village of Mercer, I felt a bond with the past; there were working farms that reminded me of my boyhood, and an active Grange Hall. I also sensed the past in the Yankee speech I heard around me.

It ranged from the high-speed, somewhat frantic dialect of Francis Fenton, the old orchardist outside of town, to the slow, plaintive talk of my neighbor Ethelyn Perkins, her sentences inflected sorrowfully upward by habit.

The sheer size of our new state, so much bigger than New Hampshire, excited both Diane and me. "Maine is the Montana of New England," I told her, and during our first months there, we set out in all directions to discover it. But no discovery was more important than the people of Mercer themselves, particularly the elders of the community. Free from the urban influence of cities to their south, they had a simple humanity and a kind of naivete that grounded me and lifted me up at the same time, making me newly curious about the world.

It took Diane and me a year to move to Mercer after I signed my contract at UMF, since we were not only looking for the right town, but the right house. I had one unmentioned question for each house we toured: Can I write poetry here? And specifically, Can I write a long narrative poem about my brother's death here? This was hardly the best way to choose real estate, but it makes clear that down underneath my excitement about Maine, I still grieved for my younger brother John, who had succumbed to a heart attack two years before, and that I needed to write a poem about him to help heal myself.

John, called "Bob" in the poem, was a long-distance jogger, and during the last six months of his life, he ran nine and ten miles a day, buoyed by an affair that nobody knew about except me. He was, in short, a wildly happy and a desperate man. His heart attack took place just after one of his runs, in early January 1986, coinciding with the explosion of the Challenger shuttle that killed Christa McAuliffe, a New Hampshire high-school history teacher, and all the other astronauts on board. On the evening before his funeral, I watched repeats of the catastrophe on television.

"My Brother Running," the title poem I wrote to pull those two events together, changed me utterly as a poet, because to give testimony to my brother, I had to make a full claim on the pronoun "I." Before I completed the poem, I was mostly confined to the third person, writing about *other* people. Afterward, personal poems in a spoken language became a mainstay of my work. "My Brother

Running" also broadened my vision as a poet. By linking the story of my brother's running toward his failed dream with the run-up to the Challenger shuttle disaster and the failure of an American Dream, I expanded my sense of place to include not only my region, but America, an effort that I now see I began in my first book.

As *Late Wonders* shows, "My Brother Running" is the original entry in a trilogy of long narrative poems published separately as I wrote them over the last thirty years, and all brought together for the first time in this volume under the title *The Long Dream of Home*. When I began to write about my brother's death, I had no idea my poem would lead to a trilogy about family. I didn't even know it would be a long poem. But the scale of my grief would not fit into the shorter pieces I tried, and I eventually found myself writing numbered sections in long sentences that swept in feeling and associated thought. The link I made between Bob's crisis and the larger story of a crisis in America set the pattern for the poems that followed. In the second narrative, "Fire," the family crisis is a fire that destroyed the inside of my mother's house, and the national one is the Iraq War, related in the poem to other American wars, from World War II to the conflicts in Korea and Vietnam. The third narrative, "Dwellers in the House of the Lord," published as a book in 2020, links the breakdown of my sister's marriage to the owner of a gun shop in rural Virginia with the political strife and dislocation of the Trump era. Taken together, the poems tell the story of an unfolding dream of home in my family and in my country.

The presence of my trilogy in this selection shows the ongoing influence the series has had on my work. The long lines and sentences of "My Brother Running" led directly to the meditations at the core of my fourth book, *Talking in the Dark*, not only in form, but in their tone of intimate conversation. For the first time in my shorter poems, I spoke directly to the reader about a range of subjects that mattered to me most: the cultural baggage we carry as Americans; the simple gestures of love I'd observed in the Mainers around me; the sorrow we humans bear even as we smile and wave at each other; our shared need for poetry; and who or what God might be. By the time I wrote *Fire* and the book that followed it, *The Ghosts of You and Me*, poems in long lines and the tones of conversation were a natural part of my work. Armed with these gains in craft, I found a latitude of theme that became a regular feature in my work, blending poems about my region with others about personal experience, the welfare of the spirit, and American popular culture, my source from the outset for the desires and dreamlife of the nation.

The main influence of my second long poem, "Fire," lies in its narration. To write the poem, I had to tell two stories at the same time: the first, about the ruin of my mother's house fire in the early 1990s, with flashbacks to the emotional damage of my childhood; the second, about my trip with her to the annual reunion of her family in the Ozarks. The challenge of integrating the two increased my skills as a storyteller. "Fire" also brought a new American place to my poetry. As I explored my mother's underclass roots in southern Missouri during the Dust Bowl period of the Depression and imitated the back-country voices of her siblings, I prepared myself for my eighth collection, *The Lost Child*, a book-length narrative of linked stories about my mother's home territory, and for the Ozark poems included in the two books that followed: *The Unfastening* and *Dwellers in the House of the Lord*.

The Lost Child took shape in my mind during a long talk I had over two nights with my mother's sister, Aunt Dot, at her farmhouse in the Ozarks. I was there to attend the 2011 family reunion and to visit with her beforehand. The atmosphere on those nights was thick with emotion because each of us had recently visited my mother at an acute care center, where she lay stricken with a second long illness, the first described in "Fire." Yet there was a comfort in the stories Dot told in her country dialect about her parents, her family and the families of her siblings.

I once wrote in my prose book *Mapping the Heart* that the ongoing model for the unfolding sentences of my poetry is the way we talk in late-night conversations, our thoughts strung together by words like *and*, *but*, and *so*, and other words like *when* and *because*, as if the sentences we speak would never end and could contain anything. My talk with Dot under the lamplight during those nights was one of those conversations, and her voice led me to the voice of my book. After we'd talked, I went to my room and wrote down what I recalled of her stories, and back at home I added others, alert to implications about today's America in Ozark attitudes toward gun ownership, patriotism, family values and religion. As I worked on *The Lost Child*, my mother, a central figure in the book, was admitted to a nursing home, and when she died there, I carried part of her ashes to her homeplace in the Ozarks. My final poem in *The Lost Child*, "Why I Carried My Mother's Ashes," completes an arc in the collection, describing how her siblings and I scattered her remains alongside her parents' grave.

Robert Frost once said that in a book of twenty-five poems, the twenty-sixth poem is the book itself. His remark seems meant not only for readers but for poets, as advice. Books of poetry should not be miscellaneous in their contents, but organized by their themes and general intent. And no theme in the volumes I've published over the years is more consistent than love. I have often said that every poem, no matter its topic or mood, is a love poem. This truth comes from my own writing, in poems about Diane, my wife and true companion; the members of my family, whom love has taught me to know and embrace and mourn; and the lives of rural people, whose struggles and dignity often pass unnoticed. Invariably, I've learned understanding and compassion from my poems as I've written them; I think especially of my most recent narrative *Dwellers in the House of the Lord*, through which I discovered the value of my sister's loving spirit and its meaning for America in a time of such deep hurt, anger, and division. That discovery could not have happened without the loving spirit of poetry itself.

Another constant theme in the volumes represented here is the subject of place, whether I've written about northern New England, or the heart of the Ozarks, or the rural South of Virginia. As a poet, I have needed to place myself amongst the geography and weather and people of a particular location to find the larger things I wanted to say, fastening myself down and dreaming it in order to open my eyes.

This is a book of the places where I woke up.

Wesley McNair
2021

Late Wonders

THE FACES OF AMERICANS IN 1853

SMALL TOWNS ARE PASSING

Small towns are passing
into the rear-view
mirrors of our cars.
The white houses
are moving away,
wrapping trees
around themselves,
and stores are taking
their gas pumps
down the street
backwards. Just like that
whole families picnicking
on their lawns tilt
over the hill,
and kids on bikes
ride toward us
off the horizon,
leaving no trace
of where they have gone.
Signs turn back and start
after them. Packs of mailboxes,
like dogs, chase them
around corner after corner.

MINA BELL'S COWS

O where are Mina Bell's cows who gave no milk
and grazed on her dead husband's farm?
Each day she walked with them into the field,
loving their swayback dreaminess more
than the quickness of any dog or chicken.
Each night she brought them grain in the dim barn,
holding their breath in her hands.
O when the lightning struck Daisy and Bets,
her son dug such great holes in the yard

she could not bear to watch him.
And when the baby, April, growing old
and wayward, fell down the hay chute,
Mina just sat in the kitchen, crying "Ape,
Ape," as if she called all three cows,
her walleyed girls who never would come home.

RUFUS PORTER, ITINERANT MURALIST AND
INVENTOR, UNDERTAKES A COMMISSION
IN BRADFORD CENTER, N.H.

In 1824,
having left a volcano to erupt
in the middle of a hunting scene
in East Jaffrey,
you arrive. The citizens

are scarcely
more surprised than your hunter,
continuing on with his dog
as smoke curls
above his head.

Nobody
comes out of the doors
of the five houses. In a leaning
shed the blacksmith
keeps up a slow

ringing sound
that dies in the fields.
In short, the place
is perfect. Fabulously
static

like farm towns
you walked through in New York,

imagining your Great
Dirigible Airship lifting
off Saint Helena

with Napoleon.
Here in Bradford Center
you begin to think
about setting free
the walls:

Boats cross your mind,
there is a red house
with a yellow door. Whole rooms
open into trees. You turn
to your assistant

with eyes that are not mad
exactly. "It's the best damn thing since
East Jaffrey," you tell him.
Then you talk about
paint.

THE LAST PEACEABLE KINGDOM

*By recreating his beautiful animal dream he was able to forget the elusiveness of his ideal in
the world, to erase his despair. If his fellow men could not transcend their weaknesses and
live happily together, the animals he imagined could.*
                              —"Animals in American Art: Edward Hicks."

Mostly they recall nothing. The bear just
nudges the cow and feels foolish
to be wearing claws and the young lion
continues on his way with the child. Still
there are times the leopard remembers.
Behind his tranquil eyes he sees
himself running somewhere outside of his body.
And there are times the wolf lifting his fine

brown head can hear a scream
that seems to come from his own throat. Yet
it is quiet here and in the light
beyond them Penn rises with Indians
as if he were their thought. Nearby the ox
the old lion forgets that he is doomed
to browse the luminous hay forever.

THE FACES OF AMERICANS IN 1853

*Let us analyze the American...The American head is generally large, which the phrenolo-
gists attribute to increased development of the brain. There are all varieties of face, though
the oval predominates... The facial features are, for the most part, more sharply chiseled
with us than with any other people.*
—"Are We a Good-Looking People?" (1853)

When you turned
to the farmhand who hailed you
from the field you could see the face
of the American.

Everyone had the face.
There was an appreciation
for the way each chin perfected
an oval.

All day in his shop
the blacksmith
swung his hammer laughing
at the nondescript faces of Europe.

At night in her home
the mother
admired the heads
of her children, already large.

As far away
as Kansas
their chiseled features rose
up from the horizon.

Indians who looked down at the faces
of those they had killed
with their arrows
wept at their mistake.

HAIR ON TELEVISION

On the soap opera the doctor
explains to the young woman with cancer
that each day is beautiful.

Hair lifts from their heads
like clouds, like something to eat.

It is the hair of the married couple
getting in touch with their real feelings
for the first time on the talk show,

the hair of young people on the beach
drinking Cokes and falling in love.

And the man who took the laxative
and waters his garden next day with the hose
wears the hair so dark and wavy

even his grandchildren are amazed,
and the woman who never dreamed tampons
could be so convenient wears it.

For the hair is changing people's lives.
It is growing like wheat above the faces

of game show contestants opening the doors
of new convertibles, of prominent businessmen
opening their hearts to Christ, and it is growing

straight back from the foreheads of vitamin experts,
detergent and dog food experts
helping ordinary housewives discover

how to be healthier, get clothes cleaner
and serve dogs meals they love in the hair.
And over and over on television the housewives,

and the news teams bringing all the news faster
and faster, and the new breed of cops

winning the fight against crime are smiling,
pleased to be at their best, proud

to be among the literally millions of Americans
everywhere who have tried the hair,
compared the hair and will never go back

to life before the active, the caring,
the successful, the incredible hair.

THE BALD SPOT

It nods
behind me
as I speak
at the meeting.

All night
while I sleep
it stares
into the dark.

The bald spot
is bored.
Tired of waiting
in the office,

sick of following me
into sex.
It traces
and retraces

itself,
dreaming
the shape
of worlds

beyond its world.
Far away
it hears the laughter
of my colleagues,

the swift sure
sound of my voice.
The bald spot
says nothing.

It peers
out from hair
like the face
of a doomed man

going blanker
and blanker,
walking backwards
into my life.

THE THUGS OF OLD COMICS

At first the job is a cinch, like they said.
They manage to get the bank teller a couple of times
in the head and blow the vault door so high
it never comes down. Money bags line the shelves
inside like groceries. They are rich, richer
than they can believe. Above his purple suit the boss
is grinning half outside of his face.
Two goons are taking the dough in their arms
like their first women. For a minute nobody sees
the little thug with the beanie is sweating drops
the size of hot dogs and pointing
straight up. There is a blue man flying
down through the skylight and landing with his arms
crossed. They exhale their astonishment
into small balloons. "What the," they say,
"What the," watching their bullets drop
off his chest over and over. Soon he begins to talk
about the fight against evil, beating them half to death
with his fists. Soon they are picking themselves up
from the floor of the prison. Out the window
Superman is just clearing a tall building
and couldn't care less when they shout
his name through the bars. "We're trapped!
We got no chance!" they say, tightening their teeth,

thinking, like you, how it always gets down
to the same old shit: no fun, no dough,
no power to rise out of their bodies.

A DREAM OF HERMAN

I was driving the old Dodge wagon
again, with Coke cans rolling
to the front at stop signs,
and you rubbing the dash

every so often to thank the car
for not needing the spare tire
we hadn't fixed. We were on a trip
that felt like going to your father's camp, only
we never got there and didn't care.
It was a beautiful day, just enough wind
coming into the back to make the kids
squint with pure pleasure
as it ruffled their hair, and your mother
patted them, saying what a nice ride it was
in the odd, small voice
she used only for your father.
It was then in the rear-view mirror I saw him,
wearing the brown cardigan he always wore
and putting on the shining bell
of his saxophone as if just back
from an intermission. You were smiling,
and suddenly I saw the reason
we were traveling together
and did not want to stop
was Herman, who just sat there
in the cargo space, breathing the scale
until the whole family sat back
in their seats, and then he lifted his sax
and opened one more song as wide
and delicate as the floating trees.

WHERE I LIVE

You will come into an antique town
whose houses move apart
as if you'd interrupted
a private discussion. This is the place
you must pass through to get there.
Imagining lives tucked in
like china plates, continue driving.
Beyond the landscaped streets,

beyond the last colonial gas station
and unsolved by zoning,
is a road. It will take you
to old farmhouses and trees
with car-tire swings.
Signs will announce hairdressing
and nightcrawlers.
The timothy grass will run beside you
all the way to where I live.

THE TOWN OF NO

THE LAST TIME SHORTY TOWERS
FETCHED THE COWS

In the only story we have
of Shorty Towers, it is five o'clock,
and he is dead drunk on his roof
deciding to fetch the cows. How
he got in this condition, shingling
all afternoon, is what the son-in-law,
the one who made the back pasture
into a golf course, can't figure out. So,
with an expression somewhere between shock
and recognition, he just watches Shorty
pull himself up to his not-so-
full height, square his shoulders,
and sigh that small sigh as if caught
once again in an invisible swarm
of bees. Let us imagine in that moment
just before he turns to the roof's edge
and the abrupt end of the joke
which is all anyone thought to remember
of his life, Shorty is listening
to what seems to be the voice
of a lost heifer, just breaking
upward. And let us think that when he walks
with such odd purpose down that hill
jagged with shingles, he suddenly feels it
open into the wide, incredibly green
meadow where all the cows are.

REMEMBERING APRONS

Who recalls the darkness
of your other life,
sewn shut

around feed grain,
or remembers your release
to join your sisters,

the dishcloths, now
ampleness and holes?
Not the absent hands

which tied you
behind the back,
already forgetting.

How thoughtlessly
they used you,
old stove-gloves,

soft baskets
for tomatoes, and yet
how wonderfully

such being
left out
shows your inclusion!

Oh, tough dresses
without closets,
lovely petticoats that flashed

beneath the frayed
hemlines of barn coats
all over Vermont.

KILLING THE ANIMALS

The chickens cannot
find their heads

though they search for them,
falling in the grass.

And the great bulls
remain on their knees,
unable to remember
how to stand.

The goats cannot find their voices.
They run quickly
on their sides,
watching the sky.

THE NAME

At the end of her life,
when the fire
lifted her house away,
and her left side
vanished in a stroke,
and she woke
in that white room
without apron or shoes,
she searched each face
until she found her twice-
divorced daughter, the one
she always said wasn't
over Fool's Hill yet,
and, taking her hand
as if they'd all along
been close, began
to call the name
the frightened daughter
never heard before,
not father or brother.

MUTE

Once, on the last ice-hauling,
the sled went through the surface
of the frozen pond,
pulling the son under
the thrashing hooves
of horses. Listening for him

after all her tears was perhaps
what drew the mother
into that silence. Long afternoons
she sat with the daughter,
speaking in the sign language
they invented together,

going deaf to the world.
How, exactly, did they touch
their mouths? What was the thought
of the old man on the porch
growing so drunk by nightfall
he could not hear

mosquitoes in his ears?
There is so much no one remembers
about the farm where sound,
even the bawling of the unmilked cows,
came to a stop. Even the man's name,

which neighbors must have spoken
passing by in twilight, on their way
to forgetting it forever.

GHOSTS

When we went there,
the TV with the ghosts

would be on, and the father
talked and called out
every now and then to him,
sitting in that space
we always left around him,
Isn't it, June? Or Aren't
you, June? And June
would laugh like only his voice
was doing it and he was somewhere
else, so when the father
turned back to us like
he was enjoying his son's
company, we could tell
he was on his way out,
too. Until at the end
he just sat saying nothing
all day into the dark.
Walking by there after chores,
we could see the blue light
from their TV, shifting
across the road into the trees,
and inside those two dark
heads which had forgot
by this time even the cows.
So when the truck came
to take the manure-matted,
bellowing things to the slaughterhouse,
all we could say was, Thank God
for Liz. Who else
would have helped load them up,
then gone right on living
with that brother and father, dead
to the world in bib overalls,
while all around them
the fields had begun
to forget they were fields?
Who else would have taken
the town job punching

shoelace holes all night
into shoes? So now
when we went, there
would be Junior and his father
in the front room of the farm
they did not remember,
wearing brand-new shoes
they did not even know
they wore, watching the TV
with the ghosts. And there
would be Liz, with her apron on
over her pants, calling out
to them like they were only
deaf, Isn't it?
Or Aren't you? and telling us
how at last they could have
no worries and be free.
And the thing was
that sometimes when we watched
them, watching those faces
which could no longer concentrate
on being faces, in the light
that shifted from news to ads
to sports, we could almost see
what she meant. But what
we didn't see was
that she also meant
herself. That the very
newspapers we sat on
each time we brought her milk
or eggs were Liz's own
slow way of forgetting all
her couches and chairs. Until
that last, awful day
we went there,
after her father died,
and after the state car
came to take June,

and we found just flour-
bags and newspapers and Liz,
with her gray pigtail
coming undone and no idea why
we'd left our rock-strewn fields
to come. Then, all
we could think to do
was unplug that damn
TV, which by now didn't
have ghosts, only voices talking
beyond the continuous snow.
All we could do was
call her to come back
into her face and hands,
and Liz just watched
us, waving our arms,
like we weren't even there,
like we were the ghosts.

THE PORTUGUESE DICTIONARY

Each morning Charley
the house painter
came to work, he left
his clenched face
holding his unlit
cigar, and his old hands
moving in their dream
of painting pastel colors
on new houses that stood
in cow pastures. He
was selling sewing machines
in Brazil, just as if
twenty-five years
had never happened. This
was why each afternoon
he looked right through

the baffled landowners,
come to imagine
their twiggy sticks
would soon be trees.
Why when he got home
he never even saw
his wagging, black
habit of a farm dog,
or thought about his mother
nodding in the far room
among the water-stained
explosion of roses. Already
Charley was at his desk
down in the cellar,
waiting for his slow
hands to come
and get the index cards
out from the shelves of dead
pickles and jams. Already
he was thinking
of the name for sky
with no clouds in it.
Or of the happy words
the women of Brazil said,
working the treadle.
Or of the lovely
language of the face
and legs and hands he learned
from a boy one night
beside the dark sea
in some other life
of his lost body.

THE FAITH HEALER

When I turned,
it was like the father

had been walking right
toward me forever
with his eyes shut
pushing that boy,
all washed up and
dressed up and riding
above those long spokes
shooting light like
he was something more than arms
and a chest. Already
the mother was saying please,
oh please, partly to me,
partly because she heard
the sound, so soft
and far off at first
you might have never guessed it
was going to be the father
with his eyes shut, screaming.
But I knew, and I knew
even before it stopped
and he begun to point
down at his son's
steel feet and whatever
was inside the dead
balloons of his pants,
the father did it. So when
he told how he swung
his strap, I was thinking
of how only his mouth
was moving in his shut face
like he had gone somewhere
outside of his body
which he could not stand.
And when he said he did it
because his son burned
the new barn down
to the ground, then shook
and shook so you could see

he was inside his body
and could never leave,
all I could think
was how the wind was moving
the tent. Lifting it up
and up around the father
who could not see it lifting,
and the mother with the no-
color dress, and that small,
still boy, all washed up
and dressed up and
looking right at me
almost like it was OK
being a chest. Which was the moment
when my own legs went out
from under me, and I woke
with the cold steel bars
of his wheelchair fast
in my hands, and shouting
like for the first
time, *heal, oh heal,*
over and over to the legs
that could not walk,
and to the legs
that could, and to everyone,
everywhere, who could never
get free from such sadness.

A TRAVELER'S ADVISORY

The main streets of towns
don't go uphill,
and the houses aren't
purple like that
tenement with one eye
clapboarded over. Never mind
how it wavers

backward, watching you
try to find second gear.
You've arrived
at the top of the town:
a closed gas station
where nobody's dog
sits, collarless,
and right next door
a church which seems
to advertise Unleaded.
Who's hung this
great front door
above no steps? No one
you'd know.
And what suspends
the avalanche
of barn? Nothing,
and you will never
escape the bump,
lifting shiny with tar.
And you won't
need the sign that says
you are leaving Don't Blink,
Can't Dance,
or Town of No.

THE MINISTER'S DEATH

That long fall,
when the voices stopped
in the tweed mouth
of his radio, and sermons
stood behind the door
of his study in files
no one would ever again inspect,
and even the black shoes
and vestments, emptied of him,

were closed away,
they sat together Sundays
in the house, now hers—
the son wearing his suit
and water-combed hair,
the mother in a house dress,
holding the dead
man's cane. Somewhere
at the edge of the new
feeling just beginning
between them, floor lamps
bloomed triple bulbs
and windowsills sagged
with African violets,
and the old woman,
not knowing exactly how
to say his face looked lovely
in the chair, encircled
by a white aura
of doily, said nothing
at all. And the son,
not used to feeling
small inside the great
shoulder pads of his suit,
looked down at the rugs
on rugs to where the trees kept
scattering the same, soft
puzzle of sunlight
until, from time to time,
she found the words
of an old dialogue they both
could speak: "How has the weather
been this week? What time
did you start out from Keene?"

SUE REED WALKING

Cupboard dishes jerk past
her head,
family portraits,

colored photographs
of Keene. She is looking
straight down, amazed

by her left leg struggling
against a current
she cannot see. O

she doesn't know
when her glasses flash
up from that depth

quite where she is,
or that her sweater
twists childishly

behind her back
but never mind.
And never mind her hair

is matted
and her stiff hand
carries its useless

puff of air.
Note with what care
she places her three-

pronged cane to pull herself
back together again
and again. Listen

to her warn the cat
"I'm coming through!"
Watch Sue Reed, walking.

HAPPINESS

Why, Dot asks, stuck in the back
seat of her sister's two-door, her freckled hand
feeling the roof for the right spot
to pull her wide self up onto her left,
the unarthritic, ankle—why
does her sister, coaching outside on her cane,
have to make her laugh so, she flops
back just as she was, though now
looking wistfully out through the restaurant
reflected in her back window, she seems bigger,
and couldn't possibly mean we should go
ahead in without her, she'll be all right, and so
when you finally place the pillow behind her back
and lift her right out into the sunshine,
all four of us are happy, none more
than she, who straightens the blossoms
on her blouse, says how nice it is to get out
once in awhile, and then goes in to eat
with the greatest delicacy (oh
I could never finish all that) and aplomb
the complete roast beef dinner with apple crisp
and ice cream, just a small scoop.

THE MAN WITH THE RADIOS

Beyond the curtainless
bay window of his house
on the side street,

he kneels
among old radios, left
from a time of belief

in radios,
some dangling fat
tails of cord

from end tables, some
in darkening corners
sprouting hairs of wire

from their great backs,
and this strange one
he has chosen,

standing on the paws
of an African cat.
The man with the radios

is so far away
in his gaze you would swear
he sees nothing,

so still you might miss
how he concentrates
on not moving

his hand. Slowly,
slowly he turns
its ridged

knob in the dark,
listening for the sound
he has prepared it for,

watching with his absent eyes
the film that clears
from a green eye.

MY BROTHER RUNNING

YOUNG MAN GOING UPHILL WITH A BIRD

Going uphill toward her house in snow so deep
the road is gone, the lover walks the tops
of fence posts. Thoughts about his dying child,
or how to keep the farm after the fire
never enter his mind. Not that he's so
preoccupied with balancing himself
in his work boots, but that the deaths of child
and farm haven't yet happened, couldn't happen
on such a luminous night, the gauzy moon
just rising over her father's roof as if
to guide him there. The only howling comes
from her dog, Shep, who has already heard
his lurching steps, and perhaps even smells
the hurt bird he holds in his coat, a gift
he can hardly wait to give. No need to hurry:
Soon, farm boy become impresario,
he'll lift his coat back from the kitchen table
and leave a creature there, dragging its wing.
Soon, cooing softly at its box, she'll shoo
her younger sisters out and shut the door
and draw him close, finding in his grave dark eyes
how well they've known each other all along.
Soon their long climb together will begin.

THE SECRET

How have we forgotten her,
the dreamy-faced girl
on this strange evening
at her grandparents' farm?
How have we forgotten
the mad aunt
who rejected her
for having such blue eyes?
Both are difficult

35

to make out at first,
the aunt standing in the twilight
by the kitchen stove,
the niece watching the way she stares
and turns to go upstairs
to her room, thinking then
she sees a woman
inside the old woman. And so,
the voices of her younger sisters
and neighbor girls coming through
the window from the far
field, she rises
to follow the aunt,
and finding the tall closed
barrier between them contains
a small keyhole, kneels down
to look right through
searching she does not know
for what—a secret woman
combing out her hair?
The photograph of a man
placed on a throne
of bureau and doily?
In that door's eye she sees
old, repetitious pears across a wall
and, reaching inside the small,
bare bureau to pull
a nightdress out,
her naked aunt,
now turning to show
in the very place where she
herself has just begun
to darken, a gray, matted
and forgotten V. This is the secret
the niece carries into the hall
with old furniture
losing itself in the dusk,
and into her own dim

room with its pattern
vanishing on the wall,
and deep into her brain
where she will never forget
the color that will one day
be her own color.
From some other world
her sisters call and call
her name, which she hardly knows,
lying there with both hands
between her legs, listening
to the shivering trees.

WHEN THE TREES CAME FOR HER

If you've ever waited
on a late winter night
at the one stoplight
of a town like that,
noticing then the telephone
wires shining under streetlamps
like the dead wings
of dragonflies, you'll know
how stunned she might have been,
how she could have turned
onto the wrong route, the one
with the ice bone
down the center and no signs,
even for the sharp turn she barely
came out of. You've been on roads
like that in the pitch black:
a car far ahead
searching the tall trunks
of trees with its headlights,
unable to find out anything
more about the place you're in
than you, looking through your own

pinhole of light: here,
the blank-windowed ghost
of a shack, here the quick
constellation of license plates
on abandoned cars, there
where the car ahead once was, now only
more darkness. She might,
of course, have turned back, unspooled
the long, high wires she went on
winding toward her around corner
after corner. But by now,
beginning to feel how lost
she had always been, she was drawn
to the odd comfort of the scrub-
brush closing around her
on a slow curve, drawn
to what it might be like not
to return, which was when it happened
down the road, way down. You've seen
how trees can dislodge
that way, one by one, and drift
toward you until it seems they're all
that moves, while you just rest
there, floating in the light. The faster
she went, the more they came
to join her. Imagine,
as she did, how they asked
her to relax, opening their wide
branches. Close by her window
a trailer passed looking in
with one lit eye. Somebody's hand—
was it a dark pine's hand?—
waved upside-down hello, goodbye.

COMING FOR BRAD NEWCOMB

The childish striped
jersey someone
has dressed him in,

his silly sneakers
upturned on the bed
do not, anyway,

matter: we've come
to see his old, dear
head blinking awake,

the pupils straying upward,
the great brow turning
toward us as if

listening. We've come
to lean close by
the bad haircut

he cannot see
to tell him
who we are—

and if this night his lips
become a thumb
and forefinger searching

for a page,
we'll ponder
the luck of all

his forgetting. We've come
to lift him down
and place him, chest

and knucklebones,
in his wheelchair,
and take him high above

its spokes carrying light
through the dim hall,
and when we pass

wheelchairs that bear
those others
like shopping carts

with lost groceries,
we'll wave a wide hello,
then wave goodbye

to the desk nurse, surprised
to see old Bradford, blind
and frail go by,

imperial and smiling.
For we have come
to this closed, loveless,

spiritless place
to leave it, you opening up
the heavy door, and I

pushing him out
into the growing dark
not long, not far,

to where the grass
smells like Kentucky,
where she and he first met—

and if then he should call
as he has called
each night when nurses come

to quiet him, the one name
he cannot forget,
we'll let Brad Newcomb be

there in the half-light,
the breeze
loosening his hair,

blind and awake
to the ubiquitous
speech of trees.

THE LIFE

There is a moment
when the arms,
sent behind you

to locate the sleeves
of your coat, become lost
in the possibility

of the garment lifting
above them. This
is why they thrash

out of your sight,
searching not
for what you think

you want, but what
behind your own back
you long for,

a seamless place
that opens
to another life.

SEEING MERCER, MAINE

Beyond the meadow
of Route 2, the semis
go right on by,
hauling their long
echoes into the trees.
They want nothing to do
with this road buckling downhill
toward the Grange and Shaw
Library, open 1–5 p.m. SAT,
and you may wonder why
I've brought you here,
too. It's not SAT,
and apart from summer, the big
event in town's the bog
water staggering down the falls.
Would it matter if I told you
people live here—the old
man from the coast who built
the lobster shack in a hay field;
the couple with the sign
that says Cosmetics
and Landfill; the woman
so shy about her enlarged leg
she hangs her clothes
outdoors at night? Walk down this road
awhile. What you see here in daytime—
a kind of darkness that comes
from too much light—
you'll need to adjust
your eyes for. The outsized
hominess of that TV dish,
for instance, leaning
against its cupboard
of clapboard. The rightness
of the lobsterman's shack—
do you find it, tilted

there on the sidehill,
the whitecaps of daisies
just cresting beside it
in the light wind?

MAKING THINGS CLEAN

One would hardly recognize him like this,
the high-school shop teacher, glasses off,
bent over the kitchen sink. Nearby,
house-dresses and underpants flutter
in the window of the Maytag he bought
for his mother. Its groaning is the only
sound while she washes his hair,
lifting the trembling water in her hands
as she has always done, working foam up
from his gray locks like the lightest
batter she ever made. Soon enough,
glasses back on, he will stand
before students who mock his dullness;
soon, putting up clothes, she'll feel
the ache of a body surrendering to age.
A little longer let him close his eyes
against soap by her apron, let her move
her fingers slowly, slowly in this way
the two of them have found to be together,
this transfiguring moment in the world's
old work of making things clean.

READING POEMS AT THE GRANGE MEETING
IN WHAT MUST BE HEAVEN

How else to explain that odd,
perfect supper—the burnished
lasagna squares, thick

clusters of baked
beans, cole slaw pink

with beet juice? How else
to tell of fluorescent
lights touching their once-familiar
faces, of pipes branching over
their heads from the warm

furnace-tree, like no tree on earth—
or to define the not-quite
dizziness of going
up the enclosed, turning
stair afterward to find them

in the room of the low
ceiling, dressed as if for play?
Even Dolly Lee, talked into coming
to this town thirty
years ago from California,

wears a blue sash,
leaving each curse against winters
and the black fly far
behind. And beside her
Francis, who once did the talking,

cranking his right hand
even then, no doubt, to jump-
start his idea, here uses his hand
to raise a staff, stone silent,
a different man. For the Grange

meeting has begun, their fun
of marching serious-faced together
down the hall to gather
stout Bertha who bears the flag
carefully ahead of herself

like a full
dust–mop, then
marching back again,
the old floor making long
cracking sounds

under their feet like late
pond ice that will not break—
though now the whole group stands
upon it, hands
over their hearts. It does not matter

that the two mentally disabled men,
who in the other world attempted
haying for Mrs. Carter,
stand here beside her
pledging allegiance in words
they themselves have never heard.

It does not matter
that the Worthy Master,
the Worthy Overseer
and the Secretary sit back
down at desks

donated by School District
#54 as if all three were
in fifth grade: everyone here
seems younger—the shiny bald-headed
ones, the no longer old

ladies, whose spectacles
fill with light as they
look up, and big Lenny
too, the trucker, holding the spoons
he will play soon

and smiling at me as if
the accident that left
the long cheek scar and mashed
his ear never happened. For I
am rising

with my worn folder
beside the table of potholders,
necklaces made from old newspaper
strips and rugs braided
from rags. It does not matter

that in some narrower time
and place I did not want
to read to them on
Hobby Night. What matters is
that standing in—how else

to understand it—the heaven
of their wonderment,
I share the best
thing I can make—this stitching
together of memory

and heart-scrap, this wish
to hold together Francis,
Dolly Lee, the Grange Officers,
the disabled men and everybody
else here levitating

ten feet
above the dark
and cold and regardless
world below them and me
and poetry.

DRIVING TO DARK COUNTRY

Past where the last
gang of signs

comes out of the dark
to wave you back,

and past telephone
wires lengthening

with the light of someone
beyond the next hill

just returning,
a slow single line

will take the eye
of your high beam. Around you

will be jewels
of the fox-watch.

Great trees will rise up
to see you passing by

all by yourself,
riding on light.

TALKING IN THE DARK

THE PUPPY

From down the road, starting up
and stopping once more, the sound
of a puppy on a chain who has not yet
discovered he will spend his life there.
Foolish dog, to forget where he is
and wander until he feels the collar
close fast around his throat, then cry
all over again about the little space
in which he finds himself. Soon,
when there is no grass left in it
and he understands it is all he has,
he will snarl and bark whenever
he senses a threat to it.
Who would believe this small
sorrow could lead to such fury
no one would ever come near him?

OLD CADILLACS

Who would have guessed they would end this way,
rubbing shoulders with old Scouts and pickups
at the laundromat, smoothing out frost heaves

all the way home? Once cherished for their style,
they are now valued for use, their back seats
full of kids, dogs steaming their windows; yet this

is the life they have wanted all along, to let go
of their flawless paint jobs and carry cargoes
of laundry and cheap groceries down no-name roads,

wearing bumper stickers that promise Christ
until they can travel no more and take their places
in backyards, far from the heated garages

of the rich who rejected them, among old tires
and appliances and chicken wire, where the poor
keep each one, dreaming, perhaps, of a Cadillac

with parts so perfect it might lift past sixty
as if not touching the earth at all, as if to pass
through the eye of a needle and roll into heaven.

GLASS NIGHT

Come, warm rain
and cold snap,
come, car light

and country road
winding me around
dark's finger,

come, flash
of mailbox and sign,
and shine

of brush,
stubble and all
the lit lonely

windows wrapped
in the glass branches
of tree

after flying tree.
Come, moon-coated
snow hills, and flung

far ahead pole
by pole the long
glass cobweb

in my high beam
that carries me deeper.
Come, deeper

and mute dark
and speech of light.
Come, glass night.

WAVING GOODBYE

Why, when we say goodbye
at the end of an evening, do we deny
we are saying it at all, as in We'll
be seeing you or I'll call or Stop in,
somebody's always at home? Meanwhile, our friends,
telling us the same things, go on disappearing
beyond the porch light into the space
which except for a moment here or there
is always between us, no matter what we do.
Waving goodbye, of course, is what happens
when the space gets too large
for words—a gesture so innocent
and lonely, it could make a person weep
for days. Think of the hundreds of unknown
voyagers in the old, fluttering newsreel
patting and stroking the growing distance
between their nameless ship and the port
they are leaving, as if to promise I'll always
remember, and just as urgently, Always
remember me. Is it loneliness too
that makes the neighbor down the road lift two
fingers up from his steering wheel as he passes
day after day on his way to work in the hello
that turns into goodbye? What can our own raised
fingers do for him, locked in his masculine
purposes and speeding away inside the glass?

How can our waving wipe away the reflex
so deep in the woman next door to smile
and wave on her way into her house with the mail,
we'll never know if she is happy
or sad or lost? It can't. Yet in that moment
before she and all the others and we ourselves
turn back to our separate lives, how
extraordinary it is that we make this small flag
with our hands to show the closeness we wish for
in spite of what pulls us apart again
and again: the porch light snapping off,
the car picking its way down the road through the dark.

OLD GUYS

Driving beyond a turn in the mist
of a certain morning, you'll find them
beside a men–at–work sign,
standing around with their caps on
like penguins, all bellies and bills.
They'll be watching what the yellow truck
is doing and how. Old guys know trucks,
having spent days on their backs under them
or cars. You've seen the gray face
of the garage mechanic lying on his pallet, old
before his time, and the gray, as he turns
his wrench looking up through the smoke
of his cigarette, around the pupil
of his eye. This comes from concentrating
on things the rest of us refuse
to be bothered with, like the thickening
line of dirt in front of the janitor's
push broom as he goes down the hall, or the same
ten eyelets inspector number four checks
on the shoe, or the box after box
the newspaper man brings to a stop
in the morning dark outside the window

of his car. Becoming expert in such details
is what has made the retired old guy
behind the shopping cart at the discount store
appear so lost. Beside him his large wife,
who's come through poverty and starvation
of feeling, hungry for promises of more
for less, knows just where she is,
and where and who she is sitting by his side
a year or so later in the hospital
as he lies stunned by the failure of his heart
or lung. "Your father" is what she calls him,
wearing her permanent expression
of sadness, and the daughter, obese
and starved herself, calls him "Daddy,"
a child's word, crying for a tenderness
the two of them never knew. Nearby, her husband,
who resembles his father-in-law in spite
of his Elvis sideburns, doesn't say
even to himself what's going on inside him,
only grunts and stares as if the conversation
they were having concerned a missing bolt
or some extra job the higher-ups just gave him
because this is what you do if you're bound,
after an interminable, short life to be an old guy.

THE FUTURE

On the afternoon talk shows of America
the guests have suffered life's sorrows
long enough. What they require now
is the opportunity for closure,
to put the whole thing behind them
and get on with their lives. That their lives,
in fact, are getting on with them, even
as they announce their requirement,
is written on the faces of the younger ones
wrinkling their brows, and the skin

of their elders collecting just under their
set chins. It's not easy to escape the past,
but who wouldn't want to live in a future
where the worst has already happened
and Americans can finally relax after daring
to demand a different way? For the rest of us
the future, barring variations, turns out
to be not so different from the present
where we have always lived—the same
struggle of wishes and losses, and hope,
that old lieutenant, picking us up
every so often to dust us off and adjust
our helmets. Adjustment, for that matter,
may be the one lesson hope has to give,
serving us best when we begin to find
what we didn't know we wanted in what
the future brings. Nobody would have asked
for the ice storm that takes down trees
and knocks the power out, leaving nothing
but two buckets of snow melting
on the wood stove, and candlelight so weak,
the old man sitting at the kitchen table
can hardly see to play cards. Yet how else
but by the old woman's laughter
when he mistakes a jack for a queen
would he look at her face in the half-light as if
for the first time while the kitchen around them
and the very cards he holds in his hands
disappear? In the deep moment of his looking
and her looking back, there is no future,
only right now, all, anyway, each one of us
has ever had, and all the two of them,
sitting together in the dark among the cracked
notes of the snow thawing beside them
on the stove, right now will ever need.

FACES

It's a challenge in America to look
into the mirror for the perfect face
as seen on TV and find yours instead,
sad-mouthed or bug-eyed or no hair
except the four or five sprouts coming in
at the end of your nose. So what's wrong,
you say, adjusting your collar
under the globes of light, with looking sincere
or interesting or distinguished? Meanwhile,
the face of the anchorman, handsome
in the confident way everyone's come to expect
from an American, tilts his hair back
to enjoy the weather girl's little joke,
and the kind, sensible face of the expert
on diarrhea holds up a diagram
to warn you of your body's next eruption.
Wouldn't it be nice to be a face,
like the wholesome, smiling woman
who comes on next, relieved of both her body's
symptoms and her body? Not you, your body's
the very thing that brought the sorrow
to your lips and made your hair fall out
in the first place. Here you are arriving
at your shit job so gorged with blood
and out of breath, you can't apologize
for being late. Here you are
at the affair's end walking the dim halls
of the subway. Around you pictures of faces
advising aspirin or a cheap holiday
in the islands have blacked-out teeth
and dicks in their mouths. Nobody likes them,
who have nothing to do with our lives
in America, the ones that you
and everybody else most want to be.

THE CHARACTERS OF DIRTY JOKES

Two weeks after the saleswoman told the farm brothers
to wear condoms so she wouldn't get pregnant,
they sit on the porch wondering if it's all right
to take them off. They are about as bewildered
as the man at the bar whose head is tiny
because he asked the fairy godmother, granter of all
wishes, for a little head. Except for a moment,
you get the feeling, none of them have been that happy
about being attached to the preposterous requirements
of the things between their legs, which in their resting
state, even the elephant thinks are a scream.
"How do you breathe through that thing?" he asks
the naked man. What the naked man replies, looking down
with this new view of himself, the joke doesn't say,
though he's probably not about to laugh. On the other
hand, what was so funny about our own stories
as boys and girls when we heard our first ones,
suddenly wearing patches of hair that had nothing
to do with Sunday school or math class? How lovely
that just as we were discovering the new distance
between ourselves and polite society, the secret
lives of farm girls and priests were pressed
into our ears. Later, when we found ourselves
underneath house mortgages and kids' dental bills,
having taken up the cause of ideal love, they got funny
because they'd never heard of it, still worried,
say, about penis size, like the guy who had his
lengthened by the addition of a baby elephant's
trunk and was doing fine until the cocktail party
where the hostess passed out the peanuts.
Their obsessions revealed at the end of their jokes,
they have always been losers, going back to Richard Nixon,
who tried oral sex but never could get it
down Pat, going all the way back to Eve,
thrown out of the Garden for making the first candy,
Adam's peanut brittle. Yet let us celebrate the characters

of dirty jokes, so like us who have made them
in the pure persistence of their desire,
the innocent wish to find a way out of their bodies.

POEM FOR MY FEET

O feet, when they called me "Beanstalk"
at 14, meaning my body was what suddenly happened
after the planting of magic beans, my arms
startled branches, my head looking down from the sky,
I scarcely heard, stunned as I was by what magic
had done overnight to you. Bad enough I now owned a penis
so unpredictable I had to put books
on it walking down school halls, I had your long
arches and toes which, whatever I put on them, stuck out
all the more. Great pedicles, those first cordovans
were the worst, deep maroon dream shoes
that floated footless on their page in the catalog
I ordered from, and arrived dead weights
in a huge box, so red and shiny
and durable, their names lasted through two years
of high school: Clodhoppers, Platters, Skis.
And years later, when I took you to dinner parties
where they were too polite to name you
and just stopped talking altogether—when I sat
with legs crossed holding my teacup in that parlor
in Chile and suddenly noticed the small people
seated around me were staring at how the pulse
lifted my big foot as it hung there in front of them,
was I any better off? How could I tell them
that I understood they had all they could do
not to begin crossing themselves right there,
that inside my foot and my outsized body,
I only wanted to be small, too? But peace,
old toe-lifters, if I couldn't accept you then,
if just last month I stood barefoot before my family
and called you in jest my Oscar-Meyer five-packs

wiggling a big toe while singing, as in
the commercial, "I wish I were an Oscar-Meyer weiner,"
forgive the bad joke and the accusations, this
has never been your fault. Unconcerned with fitting in,
all you ever wanted was to take me in the direction
of my own choosing. Never mind the hands
getting all the attention as they wave to others
on the street, this is not their poem,
but only yours, steady vessels, who all along
have resisted my desire to be like everyone else,
who turn after the hands are done and carry me
with resolute steps into my separate life.

LOSSES

It must be difficult for God, listening
to our voices come up through his floor
of cloud to tell Him what's been taken away:
Lord, I've lost my dog, my period, my hair,
all my money. What can He say, given
we're so incomplete we can't stop being
surprised by our condition, while He
is completeness itself? Or is God more
like us, made in His image—shaking his head
because He can't be expected to keep track
of which voice goes with what name and address,
He being just one God. Either way, we seem
to be left here to discover our losses, everything
from car keys to larger items we can't search
our pockets for, destined to face them
on our own. Even though the dentist gives us
music to listen to and the assistant looks down
with her lovely smile, it's still our tooth
he yanks out, leaving a soft spot we ponder
with our tongue for days. Left to ourselves,
we always go over and over what's missing—
tooth, dog, money, self-control, and even losses

as troubling as the absence the widower can't stop
reaching for on the other side of his bed a year
later. Then one odd afternoon, watching some
ordinary event, like the way light from the window
lingers over a vase on the table, or how the leaves
on his backyard tree change colors all at once
in a quick wind, he begins to feel a lightness,
as if all his loss has led to finding just this.
Only God knows where the feeling came from,
or maybe God's not some knower off on a cloud,
but there in the eye, which tears up now
at the strangest moments, over the smallest things.

LOVE HANDLES

If the biker's head where the hair was
shines in the sun while he blows
into his helmet to get the heat out
of it, she doesn't mind. It's not him
with the bald spot, it's just him. And she likes
feeling the fleshy overhang in the front
when she climbs on behind and takes him
into her arms. How else could he carry her
up and up the wild, quick, five-
note scale that they float off on? Anyway,
who doesn't love a belly? Forget the revulsion
we're supposed to feel looking at the before picture
in the diet add and remember the last time
you asked a good friend you hadn't seen in years,
"What's this?" patting where the shirt
stuck out. Or think of feeling somebody's
back, like the two old lovers lying in bed, she
turned away from him inquiring over her shoulder
with her finger, "What's that, right there, is it
a bug bite or a mole?" And he, the one trusted
with this place so private not even she
can see it, touching it, not skin or flesh

in this special, ordinary moment but something else,
something more, like the hand the hunched
old lady has in hers going across the fast-food
parking lot. Beside her an old man, the hand's
owner, is walking with what you and I
might think of as a sort of kick over and over,
but what they don't think of at all,
balancing each other like this so they can arrive
together to get a burger. The point is, you can't
begin to know how to hold another body
in your eye until you've held it a few times
in your hand or in your arms. Any ten couples
at the Fireman's Ball could tell you that. Put aside
your TV dreams of youth running its fingers
over the hood of a new car, or the smiling
faces of Tammy the weather girl and Bob on sports,
she with the unreal hair and he with the hair
that's not real, and imagine the baldies
with their corsaged wives under the whirling
chunks of light at the Ball. Think of their innocence,
all dressed up to be with the ones they've known
half their lives. See how after those years
of nudging and hugging and looking each other all over,
they glide, eyes closed, on love handles across the floor.

WHY WE NEED POETRY

Everyone else is in bed, it being, after all,
three in the morning, and you can hear
how quiet the house has become each time
you pause in the conversation you're having
with your close friend to take a bite
of your sandwich. Is it getting the wallpaper
around you in the kitchen up at last
that makes cucumbers and white bread, the only
things you could find to eat, taste so good,
or is it the satisfaction of having discovered

a project that could carry the two of you
into this moment made for nobody else?
Either way, you're here in the pleasure
of the tongue, which continues after
you've finished your sandwich, for now
you are savoring the talk alone, how
by staring at the band of fluorescent light
over the sink or the pattern you hadn't
noticed in the wallpaper, you can see
where the sentence you've started, line
by line should go. Only love could lead you
to think this way, or to care so little
about how you speak, you end up saying
what you care most about exactly right,
each small allusion growing larger
in the light of your friend's eye.
And when the light itself grows larger,
it's not the next day coming through the windows
of that redone kitchen, but you,
changed by your hunger for the words
you listen to and speak, their taste
which you can never get enough of.

FIRE

HOW I BECAME A POET

"Wanted" was the word I chose
for him at age eight, drawing the face
of a bad guy with comic-book whiskers,
then showing it to my mother. This was how,

after my father left us, I made her smile
at the same time I told her I missed him,
and how I managed to keep him close by
in that house of perpetual anger,

becoming his accuser and his devoted
accomplice. I learned by writing
to negotiate between what I had,
and that more distant thing I dreamed of.

SLEEP

The young dog would like to know
why we sit so long in one place
intent on a box that makes the same
noises and has no smell whatever.
"Get out! Get out!" we tell him
when he asks us by licking the back
of our hand, which has small hairs,
almost like his. Other times he finds us
motionless with papers in our lap
or at a desk looking into a humming
square of light. Soon the dog understands
we are not looking, exactly, but sleeping
with our eyes open, then goes to sleep
himself. Is it us he cries out to,
moving his legs somewhere beyond
the rooms where we spend our lives?
We don't think to ask, upset
as we are in the end with the dog,

who has begun throwing the old,
shabby coat of himself down on every
floor or rug in the apartment, sleep,
we say, all that damn dog does is sleep.

VOICELESS

The swelling
that starts under the eye
of the mother rising
for third shift, then
turns into a welt.

The slow steps
of the ill man's hand
up the banister
as he climbs, listening
to his quickening heart.

The silence of cats
watching the old woman
in a bathrobe explain to them
how everyone loved her
in the red dress.

The still chest of the wife
who has learned
not to have feelings
so her vigilant husband
will not know them.

The bowed head
of the boy set apart
from the others
in his chair
as if in prayer.

The face nobody sees
on the glass door
of the cooler, not even
the one who opens it to stock
cases, night after night.

WATCH

Do you remember the teachers who refused
to accept the papers we passed in late?
Their classes ended with bells that rang
again and again until we couldn't hear them

because they were inside us. We were prepared
then for our Christmas watch, whose name
came from what grownups did with theirs,
checking them to determine how much longer

they had for one thing before they started
the next. How soon we learned to translate
its tiny codes of angles into days, then years
of work, weeks off, and mortgage payments,

not realizing at first that the watch we wore
was watching us back, like a small,
unblinking eye, except it didn't really
care whether it saw us or not, mechanical and dead

as it was. Nobody could teach us that all
that time, there was this delicate ticking
on the other side of our wrists, mysterious
in its origin, different for each of us, and alive.

HISTORY OF TALKING ON THE PHONE

Once the phone, called the "telephone,"
was a voice one heard by pressing
what looked like a stethoscope
to one's ear, answering by shouting
at a device on the wall.

This was before talking on the phone
was invented—a more intimate exchange
using a receiver that allowed one to speak
to the voice while holding it in the hand.

Everyone held it and spoke to it.

In stereoscope movies of the period, starlets
lounged on beds talking on the phone
as they stroked its long cord. Men in high-rise
offices commanded, "Put her through!"

or sat up in bed on a split screen
talking on phones that matched their pajamas.

In the small towns of America, the tender gesture
of hunching one shoulder to talk on the phone
became popular with housewives washing dishes

and men in the workplace, whose big shoulders
balancing the voice, as they smiled and talked to it

while turning the pages of a parts catalog
or toweling grease from their hands,

made a poignant moment
in the history of talking on the phone.

In the cities, meanwhile, where phones
had begun to resemble miniature

PC keyboards, so square and flat
not even teenagers practicing on private lines
in their rooms could quite balance them,

talking on the phone rapidly advanced
to contacting someone on the phone,
or explaining what one wanted into a machine.

The voice, now a filed message,
was what one listened to all alone,

like the starlet in the movie
coming home all smiles after a week away
to the ominous dark of her apartment
and releasing voices

until she gets to the one
she can hardly believe and plays it

over and over, unable to stop crying.

THE INVENTION OF THE PRESENT

Encounter groups about the present sprang up
even in rural areas. People learned
to laugh together and let go
of empty relationships. Everybody held hands.

In religious shows on TV fat women
with rouge like bruises on their cheeks
and men in silver wigs who looked dead
sang never mind about yesterday,

Jesus loves you as you are. Operators are standing by
scrolled left to right under their feet.
On TV someone was always standing by
or shooting somebody or being shot

or telling jokes or saying don't delay
and be sure to act now. For suddenly,
it seemed to be all the present all the time.
Yet not even the present just happened

without the contributions of a number
of pioneers: Cher, for instance,
who experimented with gels and plastic surgery
to develop a face impervious to change;

or the journalist who brought history into the present
by discovering that a bill signed
in Washington or a good day on Wall Street
are actually "historic moments";

or the manufacturers of automobiles
that made the future as near
as the neighborhood showroom.
For lacking them—and the creators

of multi-tasking and email,
and the first voyagers into cyberspace,
bringing to that starless darkness
websites, on all the time at the same time—

we would never have known
that the whole idea of the past
would be a thing of the past;
we would never have had, in short, today.

SMOKING

Once, when cigarettes meant pleasure
instead of death, before Bogart
got lung cancer and Bacall's
voice, called "smoky," fell

into the gravel of a lower octave,
people went to the movies just
to watch the two of them smoke.
Life was nothing but a job,

Bogart's face told us, expressionless
except for the recurrent grimace.
Then it lit up with the fire
he held in his hands and breathed

into himself with pure enjoyment
until each word he spoke afterward
had its own tail of smoke.
When he offered a cigarette

to Bacall, she looked right at him,
took it into her elegant mouth
and inhaled while its smoke curled
and tangled with his. After the show,

just to let their hearts race and taste
what they'd seen for themselves,
the audiences felt in purses,
shirt pockets, and even inside

the sleeves of T-shirts where packs
of cigarettes were folded, by a method
now largely forgotten. "Got a light?"
somebody would say, "Could I bum

one of yours?" never thinking
that two of the questions most
asked by Americans everywhere
would undo themselves and disappear

like the smoke that rose between
their upturned fingers,

unwanted in a new nation
of smoke-free movie theaters,

malls and restaurants, where politicians
in every state take moral positions
against cigarettes so they can tax them
for their favorite projects. Just fifty

years after Bogart and Bacall, smoking
is mostly left in the hands of waitresses
huddled outside fancy inns, or old
clerks on the night shift in mini-marts,

or hard-hats from the road crew
on a coffee-break around the battered
tailgate of a sand truck—all paying
on installment with every drag

for bridges and schools. Yet who else
but these, who understand tomorrow
is only more debt, and know better
than Bogart that life is work,

should be trusted with this pleasure
of the tingling breath they take today,
these cigarettes they bum and fondle,
calling them affectionate names

like "weeds" and "cancer sticks," holding
smoke and fire between their fingers
more casually than Humphrey Bogart
and blowing it into death's eye.

MASSIVE

They never guessed
the dead man had something

74

so large as that
in him, yet each day

walking past their doors
down the long, fluorescent
hall toward his, he had been
carrying this

crisis about to happen,
this statement so massive
that making it
took everything he had.

All morning they gathered
outside the identical
hums of their offices,
uncertain what it meant

that he of all people,
the one they hardly knew
with the small, benign wave,
had caused the absence

they felt now in every memo,
policy, and deadline,
had gone and left
behind something so big.

AN EXECUTIVE'S AFTERLIFE

The others in hell can't believe he's allowed
to go free for eternity. Part of their punishment
as they sit beside the fire in chains is to watch him
pass by. His punishment, after a life of having all
the answers, is to have none whatsoever and keep
bumping into people who ask him questions:
his wife, for instance, here because she never dared

ask him any, choosing to die a slow death instead.
"How are you?" is all she has to say to make him turn,
always for the first time, to discover her with no
coiffure and ashes on her face. Under his hand,
which never leaves his chest, the pain feels like
the beginnings of the coronary that killed him,
and it only gets worse when he sees the son he bullied,
an old man in chains. Unable to leave the comfort
of his father's wealth and realize himself, rich
or poor, the son now kneels at the flames trying
to get warm with no result forever. He's too intent
to ask his question, which the father, on his way,
already knows: "Why did you do this?" Soon he walks
past former doormen, bellhops, and bag ladies
who can't wait to ask him the one thing that makes
their day, even in hell: "Who do you think you are?"
Nobody's nice, except the stewardess from first-class.
She liked serving passengers with expensive suits
and watches so much, she must seek them out
with her eternally nice smile to inquire, "Would you
like something to drink?" She has no drinks,
of course, this is hell, after all, so he's left to suffer
his unquenchable thirst, not a hurt or absence
he feels in the throat, but there under his hand,
in his sensitive and innocent heart, which the devil,
to give him his due, went nearly to heaven to find.

THE RULES OF THE NEW CAR

After I got married and became
the stepfather of two children, just before
we had two more, I bought it, the bright
blue sorrowful car that slowly turned
to scratches and the flat black spots
of gum in the seats and stains impossible
to remove from the floor mats. Never again,
I said as our kids, four of them by now,

climbed into the new car. This time,
there will be rules. The first to go
was the rule I made for myself about
cleaning it once a week, though why,
I shouted at the kids in the rear view mirror,
should I have to clean it if they would just
remember to fold their hands. Three years
later, it was the same car I had before,
except for the dent my wife put in the grille
when, ignoring the regulation about snacks,
she reached for a bag of chips on her way
home from work and hit a tow truck. Oh,
the ache I felt for the broken rules,
and the beautiful car that had been lost,
and the car that we now had, on soft
shocks in the driveway, still unpaid for.
Then one day, for no particular reason except
that the car was loaded down with wood
for the fireplace at my in-laws' camp
and groceries and sheets and clothes
for the week, my wife in the passenger seat,
the dog lightly panting beside the kids in the back,
all innocent anticipation, waiting for me
to join them, I opened the door to my life.

GOODBYE TO THE OLD LIFE

Goodbye to the old life,
to the sadness of rooms
where my family slept as I sat

late at night on my island
of light among papers.
Goodbye to the papers

and to the school for the rich
where I drove them, dressed up
in a tie to declare who I was.

Goodbye to all the ties
and to the life I lost
by declaring, and a fond goodbye

to the two junk cars that lurched
and banged through the campus
making sure I would never fit in.

Goodbye to the finest campus
money could buy, and one
final goodbye to the paycheck

that was always gone
before I got it home.
Farewell to the home,

and a heartfelt goodbye
to all the tenants who rented
the upstairs apartment,

particularly Mrs. Doucette,
whose washer overflowed
down the walls of our bathroom

every other week, and Mr. Green,
determined in spite of the evidence
to learn the electric guitar.

And to you there, the young man
on the roof adjusting the antenna
and trying not to look down

on how far love has taken you,
and to the faithful wife
in the downstairs window

shouting, "That's as good
as we're going to get it,"
and to the four hopeful children

staying with the whole program
despite the rolling picture
and the snow—goodbye,

wealth and joy to us all
in the new life, goodbye!

DRIVING NORTH IN WINTER

All the way to Mercer these
rooms left out
in the dark—

lamplight and two chairs
the old couple sit
reading in,

a table where a family
comes together
for dinner—

the rest of the houses, one
with the night. How
blessed they are,

the man hanging his ordinary
coat in the small world
of a kitchen,

the woman turning to her cupboard,
both of them held
from the cold

and the vastness by nothing
but trusting
inattention

and one beam of light,
like us passing by
in the darkness,

you napping, me wide awake
and grateful for this
moment

we've also been given, apart
in our way of being
together, living

in the light.

CHARLES BY ACCIDENT

Named Charlie for the relaxed
companionship we expected,
he became Charles for his butler-like
obedience, though he went off-duty

the morning my wife walked back
from the mailbox watching him toss
what looked like a red sock
gloriously into the air,

seeing it was actually the cardinal
she had been feeding all winter.

Why did she scream like that
was the question his whole,

horrified body seemed to ask, just
before he disappeared, back soon
at the door, black coat, white collar,
all ready to serve us: who was

that other dog, anyway? Who,
on the other hand, was this one,
chosen at the pound for his breed
and small size, now grown into three

or four different kinds of large
dogs stuck together. It wasn't his fault,
of course, that in the end he wasn't
Charlie, or even, considering the way

he barked at guests and sniffed them,
Charles exactly. Besides, it couldn't
have been easy to be whatever
sort of dog he was. Part retriever,

he spent his winters biting ice,
and summers dirt out of his tufted paws.
Part Collie, all he ever got to herd
were two faux sheep: a wire-haired terrier

that bit him back and a cat that turned
and ran up trees. An accidental sheep-dog,
Charles by accident, and our dog only
after he'd been disowned, he understood

that life is all missed connections
and Plan B—the reason why, perhaps,
no one could quite pat him or say
good boy enough, and why sometimes,

asleep, he mourned, working his legs
as if running to a place he could never
reach, beyond Charles or any other
way we could think of to call him.

TOWN LIMITS

1 ～

How shy she became when she saw them
outside her kitchen window—her young,
married sister leading the minister's wife
straight up the front walk. How the two
of them, noticing steam over the dishpan,
called and called. How embarrassed
she was when they opened the pantry door
at last and found her, looking up at them
beside her dog, unable to still her heart.

2 ～

The substitute, far off
at the pulpit, asks who
is new today in church,
then raises his hand.
Nobody laughs. It is his voice
that dazes them, a breezy
lighthearted tone for a joke,
an earnest tone for sympathizing
with their need, a helpless
tone for asking God
to assist them. Up close
after the service as they shake
his hand and look into
his evasive eye, they see
the voice is how
he protects himself from them.

3 🙰

"A man's property," was what he called his three-
acre lot when they complained about the mess,
and he placed one of his junk machines next
to the road where he said neighbors were driving
on his lawn. There were just ten years of cutting
down trees and dragging a rusty harrow
over the roots and skinning off topsoil from the hill
to build up the yard, before the house went quiet
and the rumors started. When they saw him
at town meeting, pale, and skinnier than ever,
even his neighbors felt sorry to see the new
look in his eye which said he had no anger left
about being a have-not: that he never owned a thing.

4 🙰

If this was all
there was to winning
the old farmer's praise,
the boy didn't mind
taking up the grain bag
by the barn post.
It wasn't heavy,
and the newborn kittens
hardly made a sound
as he swung it
and swung it, then
laid it down still
between them, not knowing
he would never let it go.

5 🙰

"Pink, and here in the bedroom,
of all places," the new owners say
to guests touring their house,

"the plumbing coming up through
these beautiful wide-board floors,"

where now there is no trace of the toilet
that old Frank put in beside Bernice,
who was by then too sick to get up
from her bed and use the flush
she'd always dreamed of, and woke

sometimes thinking it *was* a dream,
this seat above a bowl of water
you could release with a small, delicate
handle, right indoors, and called Frank
to make him do it, and said it was beautiful.

6 ❧

When he spoke to neighbors
and friends, casual in his authority,
the wife was mostly quiet.
"You left out the important part,"
she sometimes said, while he
brushed her aside and went on.
"But that time you took the car
to Canada, I was there with you."

When they talked about their dogs,
male and female terriers, she
was in charge of the conversation.
"Sometimes she actually
bites him for ignoring her.
You should see him follow her
around then. He sleeps with his head
touching hers, all night long."

7 ⁊

The trouble with Hunts is
that when they tell about
what somebody did
to somebody else, you never
know if the somebody did it
or if the other somebody
or somebody else
entirely did it
or should have done it
or would have, though what it
was whoever it was did it
was only something like it
really was or might have been,
or nothing at all like it,
or just nothing, nothing at all.

8 ⁊

It's not so amazing that Francis
has used his eighty-four-year-
old lungs all morning
to blow a saxophone

with old Cunliffe on the bagpipes,
or that, stopping his car
to lean out the window and talk,
he hardly strains the seat belt

his dog ate most of,
or that underneath
its skinny band
he's wearing a Florida shirt

he got out of the clothes closet
in his old house across the road

from the new house he moved into
twelve years back; what's amazing

is his ability to tell you all
about it in give or take one minute,
including three or four pauses
with yups and a good-bye wave.

THE GHOSTS OF YOU AND ME

THE BOY CARRYING THE FLAG

Once, as the teenage boy marched up
and down the gutter with the wide blade
of a shovel above his head, and the goats
turned toward him in their stalls
undoing with their blats the band
music he held in his mind,

his stepfather, who had only asked,
for Christ's sake, to have the barn
cleaned out, rested his hand
on his hip in the doorway.
The boy would not have guessed
when he marched in his first parade

that he carried the flag for his stepfather,
or for his angry mother, also raised
for work and self-denial
during the Depression. Seeing him
dressed up like that to leave her stuck
on a failing farm with chores

as she'd been stuck when she was just
his age, his mother remembered he forgot
to feed the chickens and refused
to drive him to the football game.
The old barns and dead cornfields
along the road in the sunless cold

had never seen a hitch-hiker in red
wearing spats and lifting a white-
gloved thumb. Everyone stared
from the cars that passed him by,
and when at last he jumped down
from the door of a semi, the whole

marching band waiting in formation
by the buckling steps of the school
and Mr. Paskevitch, whose hands
twitched worse than ever, watched him
walk across the lawn looking
down at his size-fourteen black shoes.

Just one year from now, Paskevitch
would suffer a nervous breakdown
he would never return from,
but today, he raised the baton
to begin the only thing on earth
that could steady his hands, and the boy,

taller than the others, took his position
in the color guard to carry the flag
for Paskevitch, and for the sergeant-
at-arms, Pete LaRoche, so upset
by the hold-up he was screaming
his commands. For this first parade

belonged to LaRoche, too, and to O'Neill,
another son of immigrants, hoisting
the school colors, and to the rifle-bearers,
Wirkkala and Turco, the fat kid
who squinted helplessly against the wind.
Marching with a shuffle, Turco was already

resigned to his life in the shoe shop,
but this was before he went to work
on the night shift and drank all day,
and before Ann Riley, the head majorette
following the boy past the stopped
traffic kicking up her lovely legs,

got pregnant by the quarterback
and was forced to drop out
of the senior class. In this moment

of possibility in the unforgiving 1950s,
she wore nobody's ring around
her neck, and the boy imagined

how easily she had forgiven him
his lateness, and the times his mind
wandered and he fell out of step.
For in his secret heart he carried
the flag for Ann as he marched onto
the football field, leaving the town

with its three factories and wasted
farms far behind. There were La Roche's
and O'Neill's mothers, on their day off
from the flock mill, and there
were the fathers in their shop-pants,
and the classmates in school jackets,

and the teachers who looked strange
without their ties, all applauding
and shouting while the band, capped,
plumed, and lifting up the shining bells
of their instruments, marched by—
all here on this dark and windy day

to watch the quarterback, Joe Costello,
Ann's lover-to-be, lead them into the sun,
as were the band and the tallest boy
in the color guard himself,
carrying the stars and stripes
for everyone who was here

and not here in this broken town,
and for the hope in the uncertain
promise that struggled
against his hand as he marched
to his place in the bleachers
among these, his fellow Americans.

KUHRE'S FARM

Oh where is the oval mirror that held
each face above the wash-basin
in the great kitchen, and where are the faces

of Rick, the hired man with no teeth
who drew the long, black comb
out of his overalls, proud of his hair,
and Andrew, the big, gentle son, who stooped
at the mirror and all the doorways

of that house, and his father, old Kuhre,
leaning on one crutch to watch himself
pass the washcloth slowly across the eyeless
right side of his face? And what
has happened to the room we entered then

to fold our hands before the covered
dishes and gravy boats of the last
dinners at noon in Cornish, New Hampshire,

while Kuhre's aged bride-by-mail
from the old country, who had left him
long ago for the risen Christ, spoke words
half in Danish for Him only,

and the old man seated at my left, stared
straight ahead with the eye he did not have,
eerily there and not there? Each day

on Kuhre's farm the cows walked slowly
out to the fields in their dream
of going out to the fields and each night
they dreamed of me waving my skinny arms

calling them back to the whitewashed,
cobwebby barn, as I call them now,

latching them in their long row of stalls
where they bawl for grain, and the tangled
barn cats cry for milk, and the milking machine
begins its great breathing and sighing

in the twilight. Here, inside that breathing,
is the window where I watch the black
Buick roll to a stop in the driveway

tipping its chrome teeth into the dust,
here is Les, the town man, slipping
once more through the door that leads
to the second floor and Andrew's wife

while Andrew sits and strokes the udders
of cows to strip them clean; here

are the three of them on the night
I'm asked upstairs, Les in his Hawaiian
shirt with Maggie on the couch, Andrew
by himself in his overalls watching packs
of cigarettes with women's legs
dance in the blue light of the TV.

Oh, on all my other nights I traveled
to a lost country, taking the washcloth
from its nail by the mirror above
the kitchen's basin as if taking a ticket
at a station-window from my own ghost face,

and passing then to the dining room
with the lamp on the table to fold my hands
in the half-light beside the old woman
whispering in her strange language to Christ
and the stroke-bound man with one eye
gouged out by the horn of a cow. Yet

each day Kuhre went on walking, step
by step, twisting himself between his crutches
toward me as I pulled on the flywheel
of his ancient tractor until it began its chug–
chug-chug, shaking the ground, shaking
the raised cutter bar, shaking him
as he climbed slowly up its side

and lay his crutches across the gear shift
and held the knob fast, though it shook
in his knuckled hand. Kuhre held us all,

the old woman, the big son with the wife
who longed for a man from town,
and me, the boy raking the cut hay
while he circled me on his tractor, eye side
and eyeless side, though I hoped for rain,
and tuned my radio each night from my bed

until its lit eye opened and a voice
longing for love sang in the darkness.

Oh I am held still inside a silo in that place
of love promised and work going on,
treading and treading in the green
rain of silage that fell down
from a high window above me forever
before the time came

when Kuhre himself fell down,
losing his hold on the tractor
in one quick stroke,

and Andrew's wife ran away
from the house with the covered dishes
and the oval mirror and the faces now gone,

and I, who dreamed of being free,
was set free from the silo,
and from the endless day after day
in the lost fields of Kuhre's farm,
entering then my own life of work
and love and longing.

IF YOU HAD COME

If you had come into that room
after her stroke to find
my mother-in-law Sue Reed
and me, our heads bent
toward each other, making faces

so her face would remember
what it had forgot
of the expressions for surprise
and dismay, or if
you had come in the moment

when I tried to teach her lips
by forming small lips
and making them breathe,
first to the left, then
to the right of my nose

until she began to laugh,
and laugh because she couldn't
on one side, and both
of us laughed, you might
have imagined what we did

had less to do with instruction
or sorrow than the antics
of lovers, she giving me

her hand then, I taking it
in mine to stroke it

over and over in the pleasure
of being together in the room
where you might have come
to imagine the two of us
together, just as we were.

MISTAKES ABOUT HEAVEN

I

Contrary to what is said,
longing exists there.
Imagine the soul as one
so involved with the music
as it played the game
of walking around the chairs,
it discovered too late
that it had no chair. Having lived
its only life in the body,
it sometimes misses
the walking and the sitting down
and above all, the music.

2

Having done bad things
can actually get you in,
particularly if you have been
a parent, and did bad things
for the love of your children.

3 ❧

Swearing is perfectly okay there,
even though it's hardly practiced,
cursing being a response
to frustrations on earth
that stand in the way
of mortal service. These God damns
every time He is asked.

4 ❧

Those who deny themselves
all enjoyment in preparation
for heaven gain admission
only because God
feels sorry for them.
There is pleasure in heaven.
God is known
for the way He parties.

5 ❧

Since the basest
of human motivations
are storing up wealth
beyond measure
and plotting for one's own
future, as the sermon
recommends, they have no
honor in heaven.

6 ❧

The holiest are not the men
who once looked upward
in suits or robes
to speak to a ghost,

but the forgotten ones
who sat beside trash barrels
or beneath an overpass
listening to voices,
unsure of which to follow.
Heaven is not up
or down but a place outside
of programs. Those most
ready for it have spent
their lives unable
to make up their minds.

7 🙝

Mysteries are not solved.
The most heavenly experience
is the feeling, as in art,
of something immanent
that never quite
takes place. This is the feeling
those who go there
inhabit always.

THE GANGSTERS OF OLD MOVIES

The cars they stole looked as square
as the small-town chumps
who owned them, like a kind of house
with a step in front of the floor

and two rooms inside that had couches
and vases for flowers between
the windows. Automobiles,
they were called, the name

of what it felt like for some sap
and his family to sit still

while their overstuffed seats
moved down the street

as if by themselves. Floor it,
said the gangsters of old movies,
squealing their tires, which had nothing
to do with pretty flowers or going

to grandmother's house. So what
if the thug on the running board
with the heater fell off right in front
of the cops, they were on their way

to the hideout to split the take.
The gangsters of old movies
were in love with motion,
which was why, among the others

who saved their cars in garages
for Sunday drives, they never fit in,
and why, when they entered the bank
to find the place as still

as a lending library or a museum
where all the dough was kept
behind glass, they felt like
shooting holes in the ceiling

and getting the tellers and the bank
president out from behind the bars
to roll around in the lobby and beg
for their lives. How could they explain

to these hopeless throwbacks
to another century that life
was about the pleasures of money
and screwing people out of it

with the engine running,
not quite knowing they belonged
in another century themselves?
Never mind that the little thug

who was always nervous
about making it to the big time
finally sings like a canary to put them
behind bars, too, and forget

the canned lecture on upholding the law
in the last reel that sounds
like a civics lesson by an old maid
in a one-room school,

and rewind to the getaway scene
of the largest heist in history,
where the Boss, in a back seat
with the life savings of all the pigeons

in the heartland tucked away
in his suitcase, sits as unfazed
as a CEO off for the holidays.
See how, in the perfect meeting

of speed and greed, their black cars
hit the main street among sirens
with the authority of a presidential
motorcade. Look again

at how easily they ditch the cops
and turn their square automobiles
into spirals of dust, on the road
to the Future of Our Country.

HYMN TO THE COMB-OVER

How the thickest of them erupt just
above the ear, cresting in waves so stiff
no wind can move them. Let us praise them
in all of their varieties, some skinny
as the bands of headphones, some rising
from a part that extends halfway around
the head, others four or five strings
stretched so taut the scalp resembles
a musical instrument. Let us praise the sprays
that hold them, and the combs that coax
such abundance to the front of the head
in the mirror, the combers entirely forget
the back. And let us celebrate the combers,
who address the old sorrow of time's passing
day after day, bringing out of the barrenness
of mid-life this ridiculous and wonderful
harvest, no wishful flag of hope but, thick
or thin, the flag itself, unfurled for us all
in subways, offices and malls across America.

IT

Don't fall for it.
Don't scratch it.
Don't spoil it for everyone else.
Don't take it for granted.

It's not anything to play with.
It's not the end of the world.
It's not brain surgery.
That's not it.

I used to have cravings for it.
It's the last thing I need right now.
I wish it would just go away.
I can't take it anymore.

Why is it so important to you?
Why did you laugh about it?
Why can't you just be quiet about it?
Is it all about you?

It's all sticky.
It's giving me the creeps.
It's worse than I thought.
You're getting it all over yourself.

This is no place for it.
There's no excuse for it.
Take it outside.
Get over it.

THE MAN HE TURNED INTO

All he wanted was companionship
for his journey and a chair to sit in
while he held his pen and gazed
at his shape-shifting friends,
the clouds, so how has he ended up

with a wife and four children
driving down the highway, his gas
almost gone, holding a steering wheel
that shakes in his hands? What's out
of balance is not only the front end

of his car, but the ratio of his bills
to the pay he gets for teaching English
in high school and, during summers,
mixing milk-shakes, house-paint,
or cement, which is why,

rather than clouds, he is gazing
at the warning level on his fuel gauge,
hoping that this car with bad alignment
and the great harelip the accident
has made in the chrome mouth

of its grille will get him home.
He is, after all, just four miles away
now that he's stopped at the post office
for the mail, done with a day he only
wants to forget, and would have forgotten

except for the envelope that sticks out
from among the bills and second bills
on the passenger seat, returned
from the editor he sent his poem to.
It will only cause disruption if he opens it

to find his poem hasn't been accepted,
and even if the poem has, he could
turn into a twenty-eight year old man
with trembling hands who screams
and weeps above the whine

of scalloped tires that in his broken-
down life he has found a form at last,
the very man he finally does turn into
when he opens it.

STARS

After a long winter day of work
that left his real work
undone, he would wake

at the farmhouse on the sloped
curve of the road, his dear
companion and children

held fast by the silence
that seemed to him
like death, and listen

to the muffled *if,*
if, if of a downshifting truck
rounding the turn as the driver

discovered in snow and ice
the nearly impossible hill,
then listen to the car

after car traveling down,
so intent on how they slowed
at the unpredicted, dangerous

turn just below him groping
in their cave of light,
he never really noticed

what he saw in the corner
of his own eye, the strange
beautiful flashes moving

by reflection across the sky
of his room, each opening a window
quickly out of a window to make

its long, bright point, the stars
he'd kept in reserve
all those years against the dark.

THAT NOTHING

In the moment
of your giving up,
the lost keys suddenly
meeting your eyes
from the only place
you could have put them.

The forgotten table
and open book and empty
chair waiting for you
all this time
in the light left on.

A shade lifted
by your loved one
waking upstairs,
the sound
you did not know
you listened for.

The mysterious
penmanship of snow
the branches of a tree
have brought you
standing at your own door.

Nothing ever happens here.
That nothing.

LOVE POEM

In the beautiful double light of the pond,
our day together has seemed more
than a single day, and now the sunset

clouds of the pond's second sky stretch
all the way from our dock chairs

to Lucy Point, which had no name
until Lucy, Bob and Rita's dog, began
swimming ahead of them to reach it.
Imagine that the pond, which gradually
deepens the red of our sky, remembers

another sky, where the three of them
swim together for the first time,
unaware of the likeness beneath them.
Imagine this is the pond taking them in
with the wide, unblinking eye of its

perpetual knowing and remembering,
where all the days are one day. Here
is the loon that left behind the small, white
after-image of its breast, here above a brown
shadow is the beaver slowly moving

its nose-print. Around it is a darkening
twilight like ours, decades ago, when
the ghost of Harland Hutchinson,
on the roof of the pond's original camp,
brings his hammer down in silence

making the delayed echo of each blow,
which is the pond listening and storing
the sound away in its pond mind. There,
my love, if you can imagine, it is always
twilight, and always the morning after

the hard freeze, when long-dead Caroline
Barlach, up from New York City to winter
in her godforsaken shack and write the great
American novel, bends toward the hole
she has cut in the ice for water to create,

unknown to her, a shaggy, unforgettable
cameo of her face. For nothing in the quick,
double-knowing of the pond is ever lost,
though on this night as the wind comes up,
the single cry of a loon falls away

somewhere beyond Lucy Point,
and the reflection of the pines that rim
the pond darkens around us, and the ghosts
of you and me, barely visible off our dock,
break apart on waves beside a shifting moon.

LOVERS OF THE LOST

FOR MY WIFE

How were we to know, leaving your two kids
behind in New Hampshire for our honeymoon
at twenty-one, that it was a trick of cheap
hotels in New York City to draw customers
like us inside by displaying a fancy lobby?
Arriving in our fourth-floor room, we found
a bed, a scarred bureau, and a bathroom door
with a cut on one side the exact shape
of the toilet bowl that was in its way
when I closed it. I opened and shut the door,
admiring the fit and despairing of it. You
discovered the initials of lovers carved
on the bureau's top in a zigzag, breaking heart.
How wrong the place was to us then,
unable to see the portents of our future
that seem so clear now in the naivite
of the arrangements we made, the hotel's
disdain for those with little money,
the carving of pain and love. Yet in that room
we pulled the covers over ourselves and lay
our love down, and in this way began our unwise
and persistent and lucky life together.

NOVEMBER 22, 1963

We were just starting out when it happened.
At the school where I taught the day was over.
As far as they could tell, it wouldn't be fatal.
But the principal couldn't finish the announcement.

At the school where I taught the day was over.
I had a dentist appointment right after work.
But the principal couldn't finish the announcement.
By then, we now know, the president was dead.

I had a dentist appointment right after work.
On the way, I hurried home to tell my wife.
By then, we now know, the president was dead.
I remember Jackie's pink pillbox hat in the film.

On the way, I hurried home to tell my wife.
Turn off the vacuum cleaner! I shouted at her.
I remember Jackie's pink pillbox hat in the film.
I kept thinking I was going to be late.

Turn off the vacuum cleaner! I shouted at her.
I had never made her cry like that.
I kept thinking I was going to be late.
In one frame Kennedy's head goes out of focus.

I had never made her cry like that.
The funny thing was, the dentist didn't care.
In one frame Kennedy's head goes out of focus.
We didn't realize there would soon be others.

The funny thing was, the dentist didn't care.
We were just starting out when it happened.
We didn't realize there would soon be others.
As far as they could tell, it wouldn't be fatal.

SHAME

You are beyond shame,
my mother said after
my father left us. What else
are you hiding? I never told her
about the photograph

of naked women and men
in a cart beside a fence
from his book about the war,

some with hair at their crotches,
some with asses like mine,

like everyone's except,
being dead, they had nothing
to hide, and the shame
was all mine for finding them.
I went on turning its pages,

time after time, past
the portraits of generals
wearing ties like my father,
past flashes of gunfire
and rolling hills of smoke

and flame, to these
forgotten ones, lying
together in their secret, more
frightening than my mother
chasing me from couch

to chair with her switch
to make war against
her broken heart. For in this
place there was no running
or screaming. Here

nobody knew their terrible
stillness but me, the one
beyond shame, who left them
all naked, and returned
to find them, and never told.

MORNING IN AMERICA

What draws you to them at first is the nicknames
they have for each other and their little jokes, like

the remark the woman makes to her co-host
about his tie, then apologizes and even touches it
so she seems to more than like him, and why not,

he's handsome in a regular-guy, unthreatening
sort of way, and when they all come back
from a commercial, you almost wonder whether
the blonde who does the news might be a little
jealous, given how she keeps it up about the tie,

or maybe you think just for an instant, how is it
possible for him to watch her all dressed up in her
serious costume to read the news each morning
and not sometimes think of her "in that way,"
but when you happen to catch it the next morning

she brings in pictures of her baby, and you say
wait a minute, she has a whole other life
off the set, this is a job and these people
are professionals, the newswoman herself,
for openers, reading right through the bad news

about all the shoppers who blew up in the open
market in Iraq and the shocking statistics about
obesity in the United States, unable no matter
how hard she tries to avoid a touch of sadness
on her face, as if what can she do besides continue

to be thin and appealing herself, which is when
you really appreciate the fat laughing guy
who does the weather because you can be serious
for just so long, and anyway there's always a silver
lining in every dark cloud, like he says, for instance

the ones hovering right here over the Midwest,
gesturing toward the cloud graphic spinning
into place, and even though everybody groans

over his corny joke including the ones behind
the camera you can't see, it sort of speaks

for the whole show, OK, the rock star can come on
to pitch her new CD, but not without talking about
how she overcame depression and drug use,
and the man selling the book about his mother's
Alzheimer's has to explain how forgetting

who she was made them closer, since basically
this is all about helping you, looking in, deal
with whatever life throws at you, as the male co-host
puts it, turning between guests to his partner
while she nods thoughtfully under her hair, because

she doesn't really think of this as a job, she should be
paying the network, she says, not the other way around,
though right now they have to go to a commercial
again, not just one, of course, but ten or fifteen,
the same old thing of models pretending

they are amazed housewives or sick husbands
or doctors in lab coats saying buy this,
buy that, so you can't wait to get back
to some human beings who care about each other
and about us, and who are who they really are.

FIRST SNOWFALL

It is touching
the highest fingers
of the trees
which have longed

for it all this time,
and it is sifting down

over the store with the sign
in the window

that says Come in
we're open and the sign
on the door that says
We're closed,

and it is blowing
across the gray stacks
of lumber and the jacked-
up trailer of a semi

at Dan's Custom
Sawing, and on the Rome
Road it is coming down
on the shoulders

of telephone poles
struggling uphill carrying wire
to the double-wide
and the farmhouse

with the year-round Christmas
lights, in season once more,
and slowly, softly in the dark
it is once more

bearing down
on the old, collapsing barn
to squeeze the row
of windows

shut, nobody up
to see it fill the driveways
and walkways except
a snowplow

holding a small light
ahead of itself opening the street
that vanishes in the long
drift and dream

of it, coming down
over the whole town
where everyone
under every

last, lost
roof is now far away
and all gone
and good night.

LOVE STORY

What was opening the door
those years ago to let our four kids
one by one followed by the dog
into the back seat of the old car
we'd parked in the driveway
next to the down-hill road because
the battery went dead the day before—
what, but a prayer?

What were our arguments
as we tried to time my pushing
the family down the road and your
taking your foot off the clutch
to start the car, though instead bringing it
to a dead stop over and over
—what, but an agreement to go on
despite our limitations?

What was the moment
in the midst of our despair

when the engine suddenly caught
and you roared away and came back
for me, and I got in by the soda can
on the floor and the dog now sitting
between us on the emergency brake,
the whole family smiling

as the trees broke apart faster and faster
above our heads—what, but a blessing?

THE LOST CHILD

SIX MAIN SYKES SIBLINGS
AND THEIR FAMILY CONNECTIONS

RUTH
Oldest of the six siblings in the Sykes family, which include Mae, Homer, Myrna Rose, Lana Bell and Wendell. Offspring are Thurman, an unnamed "middle son" and a third son not mentioned.

MAE
Second born of the siblings, married to Lyle. Offspring are Sissy, Chip, Daryl and Jo-Lynn.

HOMER
Third of the siblings. Offspring are Kim and a deceased younger daughter, unnamed.

MYRNA ROSE
Fourth born, with her twin, Lana Bell. Married to Sherwood.

LANA BELL
Myrna's twin, married to Avery. Offspring are Faylene and the lost child.

WENDELL
Last born, married to Amy-Lou. Son is J.B.

OTHERS

LEROY
Son of Homer's deceased daughter. Adopted and raised by Sissy. Offspring, Allie.

ELGIN
Chip's son by his first wife, the unnamed mother of "Gratitude." Offspring, Myla.

WHEN SHE WOULDN'T

When her recorded voice on the phone
said who she was again and again to the piles
of newspapers and magazines and the clothes

in the chairs and the bags of unopened mail
and garbage and piles of unwashed dishes.

When she could no longer walk
through the stench of it, in her don't-need-nobody-
to-help me way of walking, with her head

bent down to her knees as if she were searching
for a dime that had rolled into a crack

on the floor, though it was impossible to see
the floor. When the pain in her foot she disclosed
to no one was so bad she could not stand

at her refrigerator packed with food and sniff
to find what was edible. When she could hardly

even sit as she loved to sit, all night
on the toilet, with the old rinsed diapers
hanging nearby on the curtainless bar

of the shower stall, and the shoes lined up
in the tub, falling asleep and waking up

while she cut out newspaper clippings
and listened to the late-night talk
on her crackling radio about alien landings

and why the government had denied them.
When she drew the soapy rag across the agonizing

ache of her foot trying over and over to wash
the black from her big toe and could not
because it was gangrene.

When at last they came to carry my mother
out of the wilderness of that house

and she lay thin and frail and disoriented
between bouts of tests and x-rays,
and I came to find her in the white bed

of her white room among nurses who brushed
her hair while she looked up at them and smiled

with her yellow upper plate that seemed to hold
her face together, dazed and disbelieving,
as if she were in heaven,

then turned, still smiling, to the door
where her stout, bestroked younger brother

teetered into the room on his cane, all the way
from Missouri with her elderly sister
and her bald-headed baby brother,

whom she despised. When he smiled back
and dipped his bald head down to kiss her,

and her sister and her other brother hugged her
with serious expressions, and her childish
astonishment slowly changed

to suspicion and the old wildness returned
to her eye because she began to see

this was not what she wanted at all,
I sitting down by her good ear holding her hand
to talk to her about going into the home

that was not her home, her baby brother winking,
the others nodding and saying, "Listen to Wesley."

When it became clear to her that we were not
her people, the ones she had left behind
in her house, on the radio, in the newspaper

clippings, in the bags of unopened mail,
in her mind, and she turned her face away

so I could see the print of red on her cheek
as if she had been slapped hard.
When the three of them began to implore

their older sister saying, "Ruth, Ruth,"
and "We come out here for your own good,"

and "That time rolls around for all of us,"
getting frustrated and mad because they meant,
but did not know they meant, themselves too.

When the gray sister, the angriest of them,
finally said through her pleated lips

and lower plate, "You was always
the stubborn one, we ain't here to poison you,
turn around and say something. "

When she wouldn't.

THE RUN DOWN 17 INTO PHOENIX

Some nights, Jo-Lynn told Floyd before their marriage,
she got so lonely waiting for her first husband,
the salesman, to come home from the road,
she couldn't stop her teeth from chattering. Jo-Lynn

was the sensitive type, which was what Floyd liked
about her, so he swore he would give up trucking

as soon as he could pay off the truck, but for now,
he asked, what did she think of traveling with him
in Road Hog, his semi, just the two of them,
on his long hauls? When he took her into the room
behind the cab to show off its waterbed, computer,
microwave and LCD TV, she was amazed by the space,

and it turned out to be fun riding with Floyd
in the early morning as he hooked up with 44 out
of the Ozarks and headed west, surprising her every so
often by pulling on the horn. Still, she couldn't avoid
the sad, lost feeling she got when she saw nothing
for miles except a vehicle or a sign coming slowly

toward them out of the flat horizon as the road sped
under the truck. Never mind, Floyd was always
right there beside her, and when they hit a swarm
of exits going every which-way outside some city
and she got scared, he would squeeze her hand and say
how good it was to sit by her side up in the sky

above all the cars lamming around below. One day,
to show he was serious about settling down together,
he turned with a full load right into the nice development
Jo-Lynn wanted to go look at in Amarillo, Texas,
making a deposit on the large corner lot she liked
with no further ado. Now when the tires moaned

and the wind shrieked at the windows, she could be
somewhere else, namely, the home she was planning
on a notepad in her lap. Crazy as things got with all
the back and forth between Floyd's trailer in Cabool
and the house in progress in Amarillo, she had found
her calling, no idle dream to escape the motion

of the truck, but 2500 actual square feet, including
a play room she designed for her grandchildren,
and a dog house, as the builder called it, above the door
with its own cape roof, which he threw in for free.
Floyd upped his hours while Jo-Lynn, who was hungry
to furnish the rooms, stayed home, as she had begun

to call it, emailing him about the his and hers leather
recliners she'd located online, or the big screen
recreation center she got on sale, and one night,
after Floyd had parked for the night off the thruway
in Albuquerque, he clicked open her excited message
about finding the perfect place for the bear he'd shot

on a hunting trip and given its own room in the trailer.
"Imagine it behind the plant in the entryway," she said.
The next morning, as luck would have it, Floyd spotted
a closed-up Indian museum with life-size plastic bears
outside, which they offered to him just for the diesel
to haul them away, as he put it in his email, using

all capital letters and exclamation points. After that,
there were bears and bear memorabilia all through
the downstairs and out on the lawn. What she liked
especially was how they never moved. The commuters
would leave the driveways around her in the development
each day, and in the early mornings after Floyd returned

for a pit-stop, Road Hog would chug quietly off
past the sidewalks as if it could hardly wait to reach
the freeway, yet there the bears would be, standing
or sitting in the grass exactly where she had put them.
"Wouldn't it be great," she emailed Floyd one evening
while gazing at them out the window of the dog house

where she kept her laptop and could view them best,
"to have a stream running by, so it would be like they
were part of nature in some ancient time?" "Come see

how your new Grampy and I spent our vacation,"
she wrote to her grandchildren on her Facebook page,
posting photographs of the bears, which now looked

as if they were drinking or washing themselves
in the stream she had made with a kit from Home
Depot; then she posted pictures of the play room
with its big box of toys. But this year, their second
in Texas, Floyd was driving so much there had not
actually been a vacation, and her daughter wrote back

with much love and a smiley-face from Missouri
that with all the driving she and her husband did
during the week to their jobs in Springfield, they
hardly had time to visit the old Grampy and his wife
in Jeff City. It had never occurred to Jo-Lynn
until now that her grandchildren might not come

at all, ever, she wrote to Floyd, starting to cry when
she read the words she had just typed on her lit-up
computer in a darkness that was so deep she couldn't
even see the bears. "Wherever you may be tonight,"
she added, and cried some more as she pictured him
hurtling down the freeway inside a shaft of headlights

somewhere west of Texas, because after all her effort
to create a place her new husband would come home to,
she'd begun to realize she was always alone, just
like she was with her first husband before. "Everybody
is going, going, going," Jo-Lynn wrote in tears,
"and all I ever wanted was for the going to stop."

Hard as those words were for Floyd as he read them,
exhausted in the bedroom of the truck at 2 a.m.,
well after his wife's bedtime, the hardest ones
came next, where Jo-Lynn confessed her teeth
had started chattering again, the very thing Floyd once
promised during their courtship he would never allow.

"You got to be kidding me, no way," he said to himself
about the teeth, wide awake now as he turned off
his safety lights and got behind the wheel to drive west
with his load, all night if he had to, so he could make it
back to Amarillo by late the next day or early the next.
It wasn't easy for Floyd to be traveling in the opposite

direction from Jo-Lynn after the email she wrote.
At first he almost felt his own teeth begin to chatter
as he drove in the dark, but he consoled himself
thinking how happy he could make Jo-Lynn,
whenever he got home, by putting in a waterfall
with a naturalistic pool beneath it for her bears,

and then, booming along by himself with no other
traffic and his foot on the gas, he began to get
his old feeling that Road Hog was turning to air,
and he couldn't avoid a touch of pride checking
his watch to discover the time he was making,
his best ever, on the run down 17 into Phoenix.

THE FOUR-POINT CROWN

After the car wreck that killed her mother and older
sister, Allie's dad forgot all about the Junior Hunters
Four-Point Crown contest he had signed her up for,
and so did Allie, feeling a loneliness she didn't dare
think about and watching her dad go somewhere
else in his eyes and stay there for the whole

summer, like it was the end of him, too. Finally
the pastor came and said God could take the stone
off the tomb her father had made for himself,
but he had to push from the inside. "You can't go on,
Leroy Sykes," the pastor said, "with a stone over
your heart." Then her dad, who seldom talked, started

talking to Allie so much about his feelings and how hard
he was going to try to push on the stone, she worried
more than ever. Didn't she think her mother would want
him to get some use out of the one-room day care
center, now just sitting in the backyard? he asked.
He phoned up two guys from work at the milk plant

in Cabool, and they hauled her mom's place
of business for ten years into the woods where the RV
was, then lowered it down off the truck and winched
them together, so the day care center could become
a living room. Seeing her father so pleased as his new
get-away cabin took shape made Allie happy, too,

and though she felt a little weird back home when he
called her over to his computer screen to ask which
of the women on the Christian Personals site seemed
most like her mother, she eventually began to search
each face, choosing at last the one with the brown
eyes and sweet smile who could almost have been

her mother, and besides, said in her quote how much
she liked long walks in the woods, which was exactly
what Allie's mom liked, too. But when Winona
showed up in the new cabin that fall to meet Leroy,
she turned out to be older and fatter than in
her online photograph, and there was no way,

Allie told herself, her mother would wear a denim
top and jeans like that, or boots with skinny heels.
"This is my little girl," her dad said, but Allie
was already walking toward the door that led into
the living room add-on, where she reached up above
her own .410 shotgun on the wall and got down

her father's loaded 12-gauge, tears stinging
her eyes, for it was as if her mother had died all

over again. "You are not my mother," she declared
to Winona in her mind, starting up the trap machine
in the backyard, and it felt good as the rifle, too big
for her, kicked back against her shoulder, and better

when she hit a clay pigeon and blew it to bits,
so that her father came running outside to stop her,
as she had hoped. Yet this wasn't her old dad,
who would have been mad she took his gun and
told her so, but her new, talkative dad with sadness
in his eyes, who said Winona didn't like the noise,

though he himself didn't mind it, and anyway,
wouldn't she rather take his gun down to the secret
meadow and add Mr. Turkey to the rabbit and quail
she'd already checked off her list for the Four-Point
Crown contest, since afterward all she'd have left
was the deer? Allie turned toward the pine woods,

where he was pointing, mainly to hide the tears
starting up all over again, which only got worse
as she walked with the 12-gauge among the trees,
because how, she asked herself, could she even
think about the contest knowing he and Winona
were together back at the cabin? Then a small flock

of turkeys walked into the light of the secret meadow
ahead of her right where her dad said they would be,
and suddenly she was all business, fitting the butt
of the gun into her shoulder, and aiming a little below
the head of the biggest one to accommodate the recoil.
"A natural," was what her father called her, grinning

with pride just like her old dad as Allie walked
into the yard with the large bird over her shoulder,
its wings fanning out behind her back. When Allie
laid it in the grass beside the rifle, he went right

down on his knees to spread out its wings and didn't
even notice Winona staring at the bloody head

as if she were about to be sick, but Allie noticed.
Cleaning the bird in the sink after supper all except
for the plumage, according to contest regulations,
she was almost afraid to touch the little head
with a closed eye on one side and a dangle of wattle
on the other. Then she put Winona's expression out

of her mind and thought only of her old, proud dad
on his knees in the grass opening up the enormous
wings in her own moment of pride, and that night,
as she lay in her RV bed listening to her father
talk on and on about trying to push the stone
off his heart, and Winona describing her two

daughters and her beautiful home up in Springfield,
Allie drew the pillow over her head and made
herself dream of her moment. Yet in the dream
she held the limp, warm quail again in her hand
after she shot it, and parted the dead fur of the rabbit
to find the red hole in its side, and when she walked

out of the woods toward her father with the turkey
over her shoulder, it was so heavy she could hardly
lay it down in front of him. In his shocked face
as he went down on his knees and wept she saw
she had brought the bodies of her mother and sister,
their eyes closed forever, and now he leaned

over them in the grass spreading out their arms
and hands. Allie was relieved when she woke
to find her father right there on her bed, tugging on
her arm, and she was glad when he shook his head
and told her that Winona was gone, probably for good.
Only after she hugged him as hard as she could

did she begin, in spite of herself, to miss Winona.
For all she had now was the bloody, clotted
turkey feathers she found in the RV sink,
and the gun rack on the far wall where her mom
once kept kids' toys, and her dad checking out
the back window for a deer in the south field,

which, in this very moment, he happened to see. "Son
of a frigging bitch," he whispered, meaning how big
the doe was, then grabbed his Marlin off the wall
and fired it out the door before he even thought to give
Allie the kill for the Four-Point Crown. "Oh, baby,
I'm sorry, I'm so sorry," he said on the way

to the deer he had dropped in the field, but walking
by his side in her pajamas, Allie was just sorry
for the deer, which had its eyes wide open
when they got there. "Shoot it! Shoot it!"
said her father, holding out his Marlin. "It's yours
on the second kill!" Yet neither she nor the deer,

which knew her heart, and did not expect to die,
could hear him. "Are you the one who has come
to save me?" asked the doe from down among
its helpless legs. And Allie, who had dreamed
of death, and only wanted to say yes, fell weeping
to her knees in the grass and could not stop saying no.

GRATITUDE

It was the December breakfast meeting at the Ava
Chamber of Commerce, and the blinking Christmas
lights over the crèche on one side of the podium
were red, white, and blue to go with the flag
on the other side, for the speaker was Elgin Sykes,
back from his final deployment to Afganistan,

the last of six tours for his nation, starting
way back with the Gulf War, as Billy Coons put it
in his introduction, "which is, I got to tell you,"
he smiled, enjoying the limelight as the Chamber's
President, "unbelievable to me." Seated at the head
table with his mother, his little daughter Myla,

and Ava's oldest veteran, Paul Allen Dell,
Elgin would have recognized Billy's grin anywhere,
having seen it first as a boy in eighth grade, walking
in sorrow down the school hall inside the steel brace
with the bar between his legs that clicked
with each step. They were all here, the ones

who watched him as he graduated to crutches,
swinging his legs up as high as he could
before his feet came down to rest in his steel
shoes, and when his hip healed jig-jagged after
the operation in his freshman year, they saw him
begin all over again with the brace that clicked,

saying with their eyes as they parted in the school
lobby to let him pass how glad they were
that they weren't him. Yet today, as Elgin took
the podium with ribbons and medals on his chest, free
of his portable metal cage, and his former schoolmates
applauded him instead, he felt for a wonderful

moment as if he were entering the very dream
that had sustained him for years. Still, in the dream
they were all in high school, and now it struck him how
those years had actually happened to them, Billy,
leading the applause, a fat guy in real estate,
Hoyt, in the black suit, who inherited the family

funeral home, Clyde, the bald-headed banker,
who'd brought his wife Peggy, once a cheerleader
with breasts that weighed on Elgin's outcast heart,

now heavyset, covered with bling, and waiting
for him to speak. But Elgin, a different man himself
since he'd come back from his deprogramming in Texas,

was discovering, with a dismay that caught his tongue,
his mother had gotten old too, her hair showing streaks
of gray he somehow hadn't noticed. As she lifted
and held Myla on her lap to give her a better view,
he found himself recalling how, after his father left,
she'd lifted him into her arms to sit him down

on the toilet, and held him close to drag him up
the steps of the school bus while the driver just
sat and watched. Why had he not thanked her
each time, he asked himself, with a pain in his heart
he'd never felt before. So when he began
his speech at last, he didn't address the group,

anxious to hear the town hero, who'd returned
from serving the greatest nation on earth, describe
his triumph, as in his dream; he spoke with a strange,
urgent voice that surprised even him to his mother,
who'd begged him not to serve at all, telling her
how amazing she was. Who else in this whole room

was there to stand him up on the floor of the bus
and whisper into his ear, handing him his lunch,
that the driver was an ignorant asshole, Elgin said,
or to help him into the cargo space of the hatchback
after school, the only forward observer in Iraq
who got his training by watching the town of Ava

go backwards out the rear window. None of them,
staring at him as they held their coffee cups
or their forks over the last of their eggs, laughed
at the funny way he spoke about his service,
including Jimbo Starks and Charlie Webb, who rode
the school bus back then, and anyhow, with Elgin

talking only to his mother in that strange voice,
and her starting to cry, it didn't feel like a joke.
Had something gone wrong with Elgin's mind
when the military sent him to Texas last summer?
Jimbo asked Billy the next day, taking his lunch order
at Jimbo's Dog House while recalling that his wife

had seen Elgin's mother crying in August at Walmart.
But Billy declared it was all part of the home front
syndrome, where your veteran, he said, gets it into
his mind that the people back home don't understand
the war and his sacrifice. It wears off after counseling,
he said, he'd seen a program about it on Dr. Phil

and it wasn't that big a deal. Yet this didn't explain
why Billy got so upset the morning before
about the language Elgin was using for the bus driver
right in front of the Chamber; or why the sacrifice
Elgin cared most about as he spoke, with tears
rimming his own eyes, belonged to his mother,

going straight on through Billy's abrupt call
for questions from the audience to thank her, first,
for telling him straightaway after his second divorce
from a cheating wife that his brains were all
in his pants, and then, for taking care of Myla
for most of the past year after he got thrown

by the blast of a Taliban IED. And when
the main doctor down in Texas released him
to come home, Elgin added, and he still couldn't
bear the high-pitched sound of his own daughter's
laughter, he should have thanked her for calling
the doctor up to thank him, at the top of her lungs,

for nothing. Was this the end of his speech?
Elgin, out of breath and looking around the room

at the astonished faces looking back at him,
couldn't say for sure himself, but as his mother
searched through her handbag for more Kleenex,
Paul Allen Dell, the old, deaf veteran at her side,

stood up to offer a loud applause, and Billy, seizing
his opportunity, went to the podium, threw his arm
around Elgin, and called him the man who helped
to make our way of life possible, "which is," he said,
"the envy of every nation on the globe." Now all of them,
the owners of the main drag of Ava, Missouri, rose

to applaud, some putting up their thumbs, some
going up to shake Elgin's hand before they shrugged
on their coats and headed out the door to open
their shops, agencies and companies, leaving behind
their dirty dishes and Paul Allen Dell, hunched
over his baby steps, to take up a distant rear.

So none of the others were there to see Elgin's mother,
uncomfortable with expressions of love, brush
an imaginary fleck of dust from the lapel
of his uniform and say how much she enjoyed
his speech as Elgin looked down at her, studying
her face and hair. Then he held her in his arms

and said thank you, this time for just growing old,
which had made her beautiful, he said, a word
he had almost forgot, causing her to weep all
over again in the blinking red, white and blue light
of the crèche, while Myla, nudged between them,
cried to hear how loud her grammy cried.

THE AMERICAN FLAG CAKE

Mae couldn't help feeling a little proud she wasn't
the one who got the stroke, being eighty-seven

and older than her brother Homer when he went down
in his driveway reaching for the door of the Cadillac
he loved, though at the same time she wanted to imagine
him just as he was the year before, so she arrived

at the annual fourth of July Sykes family reunion,
already underway, with peach cobbler just as he'd
always asked for it, heavy on the peaches, setting it
on the food table next to the American flag cake.
Her granddaughter Debbie, at Mae's house in the Ozarks
for the weekend from Montana with her two kids,

could tell the stroke was bad from how her grandmother,
not a chatterer, chatted all the way over in the car
about Homer being the family's best cotton-picker when
he was only six, or making twenty-five cents apiece
from the skins of rabbits he caught in his home-made
traps. "He looks terrible," Mae's son Chip whispered,

and she had to admit he did, sitting in his wheelchair
beside his Arizona daughter, two tables over
from the other veteran, Shelby, who'd shown up
from Texas and wasn't doing so well himself.
He'd had his mouth wired shut, not from combat,
though he'd done tours in both Iraq and Afghanistan,

but from getting punched in the face by his new wife's
two grown sons. "You look great, Sir," said Leroy,
shaking Homer's hand, meaning Homer didn't.
"How you doing, young man," said Floyd, meaning
Homer wasn't. "Here's a little medicine for what ails you,
Mr. Sykes," Travis said, holding out his bottle of beer.

Looking up to their uncle all their lives for how tough
he was as a soldier and how rich he got afterward,
none of them really wanted to be staring down at that
lid folded over the left eye, nor wanted to feel

what it might be like for Homer to wear it, so they went
back to their table beside the two tubs of Bud Light,

where the other thirty and forty-something husbands
in baseball caps sat without their wives or second
wives and kids, making wisecracks at each other,
partly for Donna, Chip's second wife, who'd been cooking
with the other women for three days, and now sat
in a lawn chair near the tubs with her empties,

laughing at what she judged to be the wittiest remarks.
Everybody here knew the story of Donna's mother,
so gone to partying and alcohol her face turned a dark
gray color, and some were thinking Donna might
end that way herself, but in families there were things
you didn't say to a person, storing them up

from phone calls or visits one-on-one where you first
heard them, while confessing something in confidence
which got spread until everybody knew your story, too.
Sometimes, as was the case of Sissy and her mother, Mae,
what the Sykeses knew made them avoid each other,
but Sissy took a heaping plate of food straight

over to Homer's table and rubbed his back,
even though she'd known for years how her uncle
had left his wife and two daughters all on their own
while he advanced his military career. In fact Sissy
had adopted the son of Homer's younger daughter,
just twenty-nine when she got behind the wheel

of her car on drugs and killed herself. "I can serve
you however much you want," Sissy said, as if
the right quantity of sweet or scalloped potatoes,
or fried chicken or okra, or barbequed beef or pork,
or noodle casseroles, or the creamy fruit salad
she'd made with marshmallows in it, could bring back

the one thing everyone at the reunion wished for: Homer
the way he had been, the hero who gave the family
status with the medals he won in battle and his success
as a real estate broker in Saint Louis, and who had
that look of sorrow on his face even when he laughed,
so you could sense how hard it was for him

to put his feelings aside and get on with it. This,
for Sissy, was his true toughness. Old cheerleader,
who began with a child out of wedlock in high school
and now had two more by a husband who spent his spare
time gambling on credit cards in Branson, she had her
own history of sorrow, which Homer, without speaking

a word, always seemed to understand. But nobody here
could have wanted the old, tough Homer who never
spoke about his feelings back any more than Homer
himself. Since the stroke, though, he couldn't trust
his tongue to say what it was supposed to, and then he
couldn't clearly recall what it had said. Had he just

told Sissy to get free from her worthless husband
and live the one life she'd been given, or had he only
thought it? And when he turned to discover his daughter
Kim had drunk at least one Corona for each of her four
failed marriages, did he really say her problems were
all his fault? No matter, he could see from the way

they were studying his lips, trying to figure out what
he meant, that he'd been saved from himself, and now
the Sykeses were leaving their beers and half-empty
paper plates to gather for the annual photograph
around shrunken, bestroked Homer, who smiled on one
side of his face for the camera above a flag somebody

had taken from the cake and stuck in his shirt pocket.
Then, after everybody lined up for a helping of cake
and Mae served Homer his piece with a big square

138

of her peach cobbler, their little brother Wendell began
thumping the microphone. Standing beside Homer's
table with his dyed hair and comb-over, he seemed

unable to make up his mind whether he wanted to be
a venerable elder or a man who looked younger than
his age, and when he began tearing up about the old
back forty and how his mother had to sell her antiques
in the Depression, you would never have guessed
he was born in the good days, after she and their father

left the farm and started the laundry in Jeff City.
Never serving in the military didn't prevent Wendell
from choking up about the meaning of sacrifice
for freedom's call, either, or saluting the two veterans
in the house, Shelby, recovering from the violence
of his stepsons, and Homer, shaking his head no,

while Wendell signaled his son J.B., who had the same
comb-over and beefy look of authority as his father,
to start the applause. "Don't you even think about
heckling him," Homer told the wrong part of himself,
but then Wendell, his chin trembling all over again,
asked his question: "What would Harlan Wesley Sykes,

the preacher, who started this clan in Mount Zion, say
if he could look out and see us all today?" And suddenly,
as the Sykeses wept and waved their tiny American flags
from the cake and cheered for themselves, the feeling
Homer had held back for a lifetime seemed to rush
into his chest, and he was rising from his wheelchair,

looking out over Sissy's rec room with his sad face
as if he were the old patriarch Wendell had called for,
trying to find words that might convey the pain that
grew inside him as he thought about these repugnant
strangers, who were the family and extended family
he'd always known, his brother, in love with war,

so long as he could stay home, Shelby, who'd brought
the war home with him, his nieces and beer-bellied
nephews with their appetites for food and beer
and credit-cards, and their blended and reblended
offspring, fighting over the remotes to play video games
on the two plasma TVs. Somebody, somewhere

was always doing the fighting, Homer thought,
including himself, the one who had spent the first
part of his life getting badges for it, and the rest
making money, while he ignored this deep
feeling which now he couldn't put aside, this bolt
of lightning electrifying his chest as he held it fast,

opening his mouth to express the wild pain of it,
his final testimony, that made Wendell's wife
Amy-Lou scream into her cell phone for an ambulance
and brought the whole Sykes family reunion to a stop.
Weird and scary, was how Debbie described what Homer
had uttered into the microphone, talking to her new

boyfriend that night on her cell as she toked up
in the gazebo to calm her nerves. But Sissy's husband,
Bob, said it sounded like a song he'd heard in Branson
about your luck running out, which made Sissy cry all
the more. At the hospital, where Homer lay near death,
Mae remembered a long, whispered chant that seemed

to have her own name in it. It took Amy-Lou,
the religious one, until breakfast the next day to figure
the whole thing out, how it wasn't really Homer at all
who sang or whispered or said whatever it was he said,
but the old preacher, Harlan Sykes, who'd come back
through Homer to speak to them in tongues, "a sign,"

she said, "I'm dead serious, that we Sykeses might be
on some kind of special mission." Nobody believed it

at first, but the more Wendell cried and swore that he
was prompted the day before by some unseen force
to say the patriarch's name, and the more they thought
about Homer, the old soldier, standing up to sacrifice

himself for the family good, the more the Sykeses
bonded during the clean-up, drinking the leftover wine,
so as not to waste it, and tossing away the paper plates
and plastic cups and bowls and forks and knives and
spoons, and dumping the half-eaten casseroles and okra
and potatoes and meats, and throwing out the flag cake.

THE LOST CHILD

Remembering all the sorrow at the last Sykes reunion,
when the family patriarch and war hero, Homer,
went down at the microphone with his fatal stroke
speaking the words that didn't go together, partly
to the Sykeses and partly to the dark that gathered
around them, as it gathered now around the last beers
floating on ice water in the tub and the paper plates

strewn across the lawn, the holdouts in Sissy's gazebo
didn't want to hear Faylene sobbing full-out like that;
but Mae, the white-haired fixer of Sykes family conflicts,
was sure she could find a way to stop it. Still, Faylene
only shook her head no when Mae asked with a smile,
"Could it be back pain from the walking you done
today, Honey?" jiggling the red walker with wheels

and a hand brake that rested across Faylene's lap, and no
some more when Mae's son Daryl, who'd noticed how fat
Faylene had got since last year, wondered if it was a bad
combination of the wine and the heat, adding helpfully
that he'd been watching her sweat. Then Sissy,
Faylene's first cousin and confidante sitting beside her,
whispered into her ear, was this about her husband back

in Texas, who never took her anywhere, including here,
because he was too damn busy with his hubcap business,
and Faylene, reminded by all her Ozark relatives'
attention of the sadness in her life, sobbed even
louder, crying out at last, "My father Avery
was a turd." In the moment of silence afterward
nobody thought about Homer Sykes at all, except

his daughter, Kim. She recalled how Homer never once
came home from the military when she was a kid
needing a father, and decided he was a turd, too.
"You don't mean that, Honey," Mae said, still jiggling
the walker, but her brother Wendell, who had always
believed the guy who married their sister, Lana Bell,
was a high-toned son-of-a-bitch, hoped Faylene

did mean it. Wearing an uncle's expression of concern,
he went over and stroked her arm, saying she shouldn't
speak ill of her father now that both he and her mother
were dead. This was how he got her to tell him
what Avery did to Lana's photograph album,
cutting her dead first husband out of all the pictures
with scissors, and even cutting her head off

in one of them, where the husband had his arm
around her shoulder, and now that her parents
were gone, Faylene added, drying tears with the back
of her hand, and there was no more Avery to hide
her mother's car keys and accuse her of things
he imagined with other men, she couldn't stop thinking
of a little girl all alone, as she called herself, with no

brothers or sisters, sneaking out that album over
and over to find the same holes in it. They were like
the happiness Avery had stolen from both of them,
she said, all the while holding hands with her mother
as if they were love-birds in front of his high-class

friends. "I could almost see why Wendell done it,"
Mae remarked afterward, explaining the whole thing

to her older sister Ruth on the phone. "Why Wendell
done what?" asked Ruth. "Why he got all red in the face
and started speaking ill of Avery himself—worse
than ill, really—calling him a blowhard who thought
he knew it all, but didn't know anything about the boy
nobody could of cut out of the album because
he wasn't even in it, the one that got Lana Bell

pregnant at fifteen, when Mama packed up
her things and sent her out East to live with you
and have the baby," Mae said. "Which I could almost see
why Wendell done," she repeated, fearing how angry
Ruth, who had the worst temper of all the Sykeses,
was going to be that their little brother had blurted
this old family secret sealed away for years.

"Not that he should of done it," Mae added. But Ruth
didn't seem to get mad, and when Mae went on to tell her
about how hard Faylene took what Wendell had said—crying
so, it would break your heart about her poor,
unknown brother or sister with no family, a lost child,
just like herself—there was no sound from the other end
of the phone except for the amazed, excited

voices on Ruth's TV and her radio, talking
at the same time about something for sale. "That
was when I decided to call you up, Ruth, and find out
whatever happened to that child," Mae said, relieved
to have got these words out at last. Now she felt a bit
teary herself, though having no tolerance for tears,
she let them build up in her nose so she could get

rid of them by blowing it hard one time. Meanwhile,
her actual sister, who was not the one Mae imagined
at all, stared confusedly out through her tilted

glasses at the pathways around her chair, one
trailing off through stacks of magazines toward
the kitchen, another heading past the glow lights
and sacks of fertilizer and piles of clothes to disappear

down the hall into the dark, wondering who,
exactly, this Faylene was, anyway. Oh, Ruth
remembered Wendell all right, the baby brother
that her mother had late, and spoiled rotten,
and she recalled her baby sister Lana Bell,
but now she was thinking about how her mother
had spoiled Lana and her twin Myrna, too,

giving them both movie star names, while Ruth,
the oldest of the seven kids, got the Bible name,
the switch, and all the house chores. "I am
the lost child, Mama," Ruth declared, then
tugged hard on her baseball cap, repeating herself
with more conviction, so there was no mistaking
what she had said. Soon, the whole Sykes family

was repeating it. Surprised and alarmed, Mae called up
Ruth's middle son, the one who understood his mother
had a good side, then phoned Amy-Lou, Wendell's wife,
who told Wendell, who called everybody he could
think of, more mournful each time that the sister
he never liked seemed to be losing her grip again,
and more pleased with his importance as the person

bearing the news. "Tell Aunt Ruth we're rooting
for her," Faylene wrote to Amy-Lou on Facebook,
thanking her for the photos of the reunion, especially
drawn to the one where she was smiling in the gazebo
beside Sissy and you could hardly see her walker. "Can't
wait till next year," she said. She never mentioned
the lost child, and as the Sykeses all emailed

their reunion photos to each other and searched
for the ones that showed them smiling, too,
even the holdouts who had listened to Faylene cry
in the gathering darkness wanted to be back there
once more, where they were having so much fun.
Being lost wasn't an issue to Ruth now, either,
unless you counted her struggle over the phone

to identify Mae, who called to offer comfort on Ruth's
first night in the nursing home. "I'm the sister
with the husband that died the same year yours did,"
Mae explained, then listened to the distant voices
of commercials on the TV, while Ruth thought about
husbands and sisters and women getting cleaner counters
and kitchen floors. "The only one that's still alive,"

Mae added, then wished she hadn't, because
it made her think of how useless and dead she felt
in that moment as the family helper Faylene suddenly
didn't need and Ruth didn't even know. She wanted
Ruth to get mad at her about something, anything,
or maybe to explain how she could have said
she was a lost child, when they both knew

she was the strong and independent one. "Remember
how I always went to you for the answers when
we was kids?" she asked, and finding no answer, Mae,
who never cried, felt tears in her eyes. "Remember?"
she said again to the voices on the TV and the other
old woman holding the phone, Mae's tears coming
so fast now she didn't even think to blow her nose.

DANCING IN TENNESSEE

How was he to know, when his father left them
and his mother took him by the hand
to her clothes closet, screaming

because he did not understand how to behave
and because, alone and lost, she herself
did not understand how to behave,
that this was the room she led him to,

20B in the nursing home, where he sat
once more in the dim light among her slippers
and shoes, calling out to her, "Mama, Mama,"

though now she was right there
in her bed, half-deaf, eyes wide open
in her blindness, her teeth out,
breathing rapidly through her mouth?

How could he have known when she whipped him
as if she would never stop because his father
loved someone else, it was the shock

of this final unbelievable lovelessness
she was preparing him for? All gone, her years
afterward with the new man, and the house
and farm she helped build to replace

the hopes that she once had. Gone
to ruin, the house and the farm,
but never mind. And never mind

her lifelong anger, and all her failures
of the heart: this was not his mother.
Lying on her stroke side, her nose
a bony thing between her eyes that blinked

and blinked so he could see behind them
to her fear, she was a creature
whose body had failed, and he had no way

to reach except through her favorite song
he sang as a boy to lift the grief from her face,
and began to sing now, "The Tennessee Waltz,"
understanding at last that its tale of love stolen

and denied was the pure inescapable
story of her life—his father the stolen
sweetheart she never forgave

or forgot. It didn't matter that she could not
see him beside her there or, struggling for air,
she was unable to eat or drink
or sing. He took her good hand in his

and rocked her and sang for them both,
his mother discovering once more in the tips
of her fingers what touch was like,

and he discovering too, while he sang on
and on, stealing her back from this moment
in the small, dim room where she lay dying,
and they danced and danced.

WHY I CARRIED MY MOTHER'S ASHES

Because her mother told her in the Ozarks
don't come running back.
Because it was too far to run back.

Because when my father left her
in the projects of Springfield, Vermont,

up all night sewing with three
kids upstairs, she went back anyway
in her mind. Because I looked up at her

147

bent over the Singer's tiny light
that hurt my eyes and left a scar

on everything I saw, the scar of her
rejection and hurt. Because I missed her
while she was right there beside me

disappearing into her work, then and in all
the years afterward, making a life

with my stepfather out of exhaustion
and self-denial and unrequited
longing. Because late on lonely nights

she phoned to hear the voices of her sisters
and brothers talking about nothing

at all, which was for her the dearest talk.
Because the wings of the plane
lifted me high above the rain clouds

of New England as I carried the ashes back
to the rolling fields and farmhouses and hot sun

of the country where she was born.
Because in the cooling twilight my old
widowed Aunt Dot waited for me

among family photographs in her small
apartment, and I lay right down on the pump-up

mattress by the fan. Because, when I woke,
I discovered her just as she had always been,
never mind the bad circulation

in her legs, up early bringing back her dead
husband and sister and brother in stories

where they lived with her children
and grandchildren while the toast popped up
and the ham and eggs fried.

Because as we arrived at the graves
of my grandmother and grandfather, my uncles

and their wives waited, too, Truman on a cane
smiling beside his Cadillac with his sorrowful face
and offering me his good hand,

and her baby brother, Wallace, the one
she never liked, shaking my hand and tearing up

while he called her a damn Yankee. Because
when they listened to me read Walt Whitman,
whom they did not know, asking them to look for him

under their bootsoles, all my uncles and aunts
bowed their heads and looked respectfully down

at their shoes. Because when Truman, the old soldier,
walked solemnly to the graves to spread
the ashes, he threw himself to one side

on his cane with each step, bringing his shoulders up
erect and military. Because we held the small box

for each other, Dot for Truman, I for Wallace,
who tipped his bald head so I saw up close
the wide adhesive bandage from the operation.

Because as they reached inside, taking the gray
dust into their old hands, they must have felt

it was their dust, too, each of them speaking
to my mother in a soft, casual way as if
she stood there beside them in the cloud

that rose from the grass. Because they loved her,
as I did in this moment when she seemed

to join us, and I no longer missed her.
Because the voice I heard then was my own voice
saying a loud Amen, now mixed

with their Amens, all of us bound together
in this homeplace where I had carried my mother,

who would never need to run back to it,
or dream of it holding their voices to her ear,
because she would never, ever again, be gone.

THE UNFASTENING

THE BUTTON

It's not easy to button the top
button on the dress shirt
of an old man, his chin back,

his helpless hands
dangling at his sides
imagining themselves

doing what they're now
unable to do as you struggle,
close enough you share

his labored breath
and feel the growing
distance between what

he wants and cannot have,
and the distance
has become you,

not done with him and this
small, unyielding button
even after you are done.

TRUMAN'S STROKE

A silent lightning
cracked him
in two, one leg
dangling a foot

that can't feel
the floor
when he walks,
the other guiding it,

a zig-zag dance,
and he the impresario
with his cane.
My Uncle Truman,

the military man
once so tucked in
nobody
could dig him out,

now unable
to tuck himself,
or trust his slack
tongue with only

what he wants it
to say. Yet see
him smile
with bunny teeth

when he whispers
to the new girlfriend
he sits beside,
and the feeling

that rises into
his fingers as he not
quite touches
her white hair,

arriving despite himself
out in the open,
his little death
bringing him to life.

THE UNFASTENING

As the father turns away from the thought
of his failure, the hands remove
his glasses and rub his eyes over

and over, drying the nonexistent tears.
Unknown to the one who is troubled
about losing his hair, his fingers stroke

his baldness as he speaks. The body,
our constant companion, understands
the loneliness of the hostess in her dark

driveway, embracing herself after the guests
who promised more and soon have gone,
and even visits the old schoolteacher

who reads the same happy ending to each
new class, working her toes in her shoes.
How could the people of the kingdom

not have known the curse of sorrow
was nothing more than a long sleep
they had only to wake from? In dreams

the body, which longs for transformation
too, suddenly lifts us above the dark
roofs of our houses, and far above

the streets of the town, until they seem
like any other small things fastened to earth.

THE RHUBARB ROUTE

On a spring evening in between the black fly season
and the first mosquitoes, as the red stems lift

their broad leaves like scores of tilted umbrellas,
I call them on the telephone of my mind and drive
bagfuls of rhubarb down through the town, past
the white revenants of the Grange Hall and the closed
library, past the house lots and the treeless modulars
where they have no use for rhubarb, turning at last into
a wide driveway while little Herman, alive as anyone,
comes out of his old farmhouse with his chesty walk
to take two bags inside to Faye, enough for a whole
year of pies and red jello cobblers, then drive the back
way along the river, by the oaks and sumacs gathering
the shadows of twilight, to swing in beside the dead
school bus of True's cowless farm and see old Billy,
before his legs gave out, who loved rhubarb almost
as much as his long-lost mother, take the biggest bag
of it into his arms and carry it up the steps of his porch,
leaning on the rail to wave goodbye. Goodbye to Billy,
goodbye to little Herman, goodbye to the Gagnons,
who laugh in the deepening dusk about eating sticks
of rhubarb right from the patch as kids, goodbye
to my old neighbor Ethelyn in the house on the corner,
empty for two years, who all the same calls out
Hello from somewhere inside when I knock, *Hello,
I'm here*, and suddenly she is here next to me behind
the screen, smiling because I've remembered her again
on this spring evening with fresh rhubarb, which
she holds up to her face, breathing it in with a long
breath before she turns and goes back into the dark.

THIS POEM

Before the age of doing
and photographing and filming
and texting what you did,
back when people simply did,
a girl got married at seventeen,

recalled tonight under lamplight
in an Ozark farmhouse by my old,
widowed Aunt Dot, the woman
who once was her. There were no
photos of the girl as she waited

in the truck with her first
two babies for her husband
to come out of the bar
until it was dark, and then
in the dark. Nobody filmed him

at the screen door of the kitchen,
waking from the spell
of his anger with a lead pipe
in his hand saying, "I believe
I killed that cow," or filmed her

stepping between his fists
and her son on the night he broke
her nose. Literal, plainspoken
and sorrowful, Dot seems
to find her, the poor young girl,

married for life, and him, my uncle,
the good old boy everyone loved,
including me, in the shadows
cast by her lamp and chair,
just the three of them there,

and me, and the small,
hand-held device of this poem.

KAY

Everybody in the family knew the story
of how Henry's war bride got out of the car
in the yard dressed up in a kimono
and bowing. Their father was so surprised
he dropped his pail of feed. None of them
ever wondered about the shock she
must have felt to find her new father-in-law
among a gang of hogs in the Ozarks
wearing bib overalls and a straw hat.
She being a foreigner, it was *her* job
to understand *him*. "Over there," Henry said,
they eat fish raw," and he had his older
sister show her how to make biscuits
and pork gravy. In the end, sorrow opened them
to her. After just seven years, Henry,
who'd been drinking, drove his truck over
an embankment and died in the accident,
leaving her with two young girls, and hardly able
to speak English. Henry's brother got her a job
as a waitress at the local restaurant, and his sisters
took turns babysitting. "You could eat right
off her floors," one of them told a friend,
and later, when the restaurant's owner
promoted her to bookkeeper, they bragged
about how fast her fingers moved on the abacus
she'd brought from Japan. There, no one
would have understood how her first daughter,
who looked like Henry except for her black hair
and her eyes, could have been so wild
as to jump on a motorcycle at fifteen behind
her new boyfriend, and her mother couldn't make
herself understand it, either. "Oh, Kay,"
the women said at the funeral, holding her,
for by then she was part of the family.
None of them ever wondered about her real
name, or knew how pleased she was long before

to have this one, which Henry gave her
on the way to America, where she would spend
the rest of her life discovering who Kay was.

TELEPHONE POLES

Like our cars, which have our faces,
and our houses, which look down
on us under their folded hats,

these resemble us, though nothing
we have made seems so steadfast.
Exiled to the roadside,

they stand in all weather, ignored
except for the rows of swallows
that remember them in springtime,

and the occasional tree holding up
a hole workmen have cut
to let the lines through. Yet they go on

balancing cables on their shoulders
and passing them to the next
and the next, this one extending

a wire to a farmhouse, that one
at the corner sending lines
four ways at once, until miles

away where the road widens,
and the tallest poles rise,
bearing streetlamps high above

the doors of the town, arriving
by going nowhere at all, each,
like the others that brought them here,

making its way by accepting
what's given, and holding on,
and standing still.

MAINTAINING

I 〜

Don't think you know the fat woman
in charge of the dump, married
to the one laid up from the accident
two years ago at the pulp mill,
who wears the easygoing, happy
face when you drive in with your load
of trash, calling her name. That's not her.

2 〜

By the register at the store, truckers,
carpenters and mill workers
count their change while telling
the morning clerk how they are:
"Not too bad." "Could be worse."
"Maintaining."

3 〜

Billy True maintains. His mother,
he explains after bush-hogging my field,
has come down with All-timers,
and begun calling him by his dead
father's name. He shakes his head:
a sad situation, but even so,
you can see he kind of likes it,
perhaps because in the All-time
of her mind, his father, whose death
she mourned for years, can still be alive.

Also because now, the one he's always
loved most will always love him.

4 ⚮

People here don't talk much
about love. Listen for it
in other words—how old
Ethelyn Perkins lingers slightly
over the word "grandchildren,"
or describes her new neighbors
with what seems a fond
description of her own past
in this town: "They're a young
couple, just starting out."

5 ⚮

And just because they don't speak
of beauty doesn't mean they haven't
noticed it: the sunset's astonishment
of red on the horizon, tinting the town's
downhill windows, for instance, or how
at night, in your headlights as you travel
the last mile home, the feathery pines
alongside your car seem to gather
you up in the wings of their dark flight.

6 ⚮

But what of the stranger at town meeting
with the designer suit and perfect
manners, sympathetic to everyone's
questions about his proposal to turn
Cunliffe's back field into house lots
because he knows his audience can't refuse?
"I would urge you to consider the large
increase in your tax base," he says.

7 ❧

Twelve years later his faded
sign with the lot map announces
MyPropertyForYou.com
to the ivy dangling from it
and the vestiges of a gravel road
curving alongside power poles.
In the enclosure of pines his men
planted around lot 3, indentations
in the grass show where
the deer slept. Swallows rest
on the unused electric wire
off lots 6 and 7. And deeper still,
by the culverts where my dogs run,
waves of daisies, buttercups,
Indian paintbrushes and Queen
Anne's lace crest in the light wind,
more wildflowers than in any
year before. "Change doesn't need
to be a bad thing," he said.

8 ❧

Established by vanished farmers,
the Grange Hall's now
a ceramics studio. The old school,
bought for one dollar, houses
the town office, zumba classes,
and Story Time for kids.
A single-door rescue trailer
with a giant American flag decal,
obtained after the scare of 9/11
by a grant from Homeland Security,
rusts in the back. Having survived
the Industrial Revolution,
the regional school movement
and the rise of global terrorism,
our town's still here.

GETTING LOST

I'm not proud of it, but I couldn't resist
Serena, the British woman on my GPS,
who understood I had better things to do
while driving than to think about what
I was doing, and who had the most charming

difficulty with her r's. I went everywhere
with her, making each turn she whispered
with that lisp of hers into my ear as I watched
the man she had made of me on my GPS TV,
a superhero in a blue car taking on the tangle

of roads that tumbled out of the horizon,
until Diane, my wife and former navigator,
who couldn't match Serena's expertise,
not to mention her modest compliance, began
to resent her. "She says 'rump' instead of 'ramp,'"

Diane remarked as I made another perfect
exit off the thruway, "and that thing she does
with her r's is driving me nuts." It was wonderful
to be the source of conflict between two
women, but then I began to consider how

my destination time in the lower left corner
kept adjusting itself according to my speed,
a small reminder that in the very moment
I was enjoying my triumph over the map,
a computer somewhere that knew everything

was mapping me. I recall a certain period
of melancholy before I returned to my wife,
Serena and I had been that good together,
I having made so many wrong turns
in my life, she only wanting to help me

make them right. Yet I couldn't stop longing for,
of all things, the fights Diane and I once had
about the urgency of finding our way,
and the seductive thought of ending up
beside some forgotten field among cows

on a dwindling road that didn't even exist
on the ragged copy of the known world
she held in her lap. Which was, minus the cows,
just where we were one week after I unplugged
the GPS, and we sat quietly at the roadside

spent by our argument, she turning to me
with her blue eyes and that old, dear expression
of helplessness, I falling in love all over again
because there was no Serena to recalculate,
only the two of us together once more, getting lost.

PRAISE SONG

There was no stopping the old pear tree
in our backyard. After we released it
from a staked cord, it stood on the lawn
for a month as if coming to its decision
to lie back down on the ground again.
All winter we left it for dead, but in the spring
it lay in an island of unmowed grass
blooming beside its mate, and this May,
when I separate their branches
and look in, I find new shoots and flowers.

At the end of my life I want to lie down
in the long grass with one arm by my side
lifting me up as I reach out to her with all the others
and she reaches back. I want to know nothing
but the humming and fumbling of bees

carrying seed dust on their bellies from my blossoms
to her blossoms in the dome of green shade.

BENEDICTION

Consider the lilies of the field,
how they grow
beyond their flowering, no longer
beautiful to our eyes. Consider
the brittle-petalled, black
centers of the black-eyed Susans,
waving like pom-poms
in the cold wind. There's a joy in it,
the joy of everything
that dances around it,
the milkweeds dangling their old,
goose-bumpy pods,
the Queen Anne's Lace
lifting the lacy purses
they have woven
from their blossoms. How could we
have overlooked the beauty
of the tiny, bristled stars
they now carry, or the hope,
among the brown clovers,
of the late bloomers, already living
the dream of their return?
Consider the dream
of the bloomers and of the wind-
torn blackberry bushes
holding out their stick fingers
that the birds have picked
clean. Consider the frosted heads
of the goldenrods
bending down to the ground,
and the milkweeds standing
straight up, giving themselves away.

THE LONG DREAM OF HOME: A TRILOGY

To bring right order to the world, we must find right order in the nation;
to bring order to the nation, we must find order in the family;
to bring order to the family, we must cultivate our personal life;
we must set our hearts right.
—Confucius

PART ONE

MY BROTHER RUNNING

I ↝

It is impossible to stop my brother.
In my fantasy, everyone tries. My mother comes
from the nursery and truck garden
she never wanted but inherited anyway after
my stepfather's death. "Look what happened
to me," she says to him. "Work, work,
work, the whole place growing up
into trees. For once in this family think
what you're getting yourself into."

Our older brother Jim flies in from Alaska.
"Here I am," he says, "shuffling
around in Mukluks with a truss on
under my jeans and a shot liver
from drinking too many 12-packs.
So much for my big dream of finding the home
where I belong on the frontier.
Forget this running shit. It won't
get you where you want to go, either."

The truth is, nobody tries to stop him.
My mother, fresh out of solutions,
is raising chinchillas to save the farm
and show the world how much she cared
about her husband all along.
Against doctor's orders, Jim
is probably cracking beers for himself
and this guy he has just met, a real
find, one of the sharpest characters in Sitka.

I'm not even there, not yet, off in my own
world, no doubt, writing poems.
So there Bob is by himself,
unaware I am now discovering him
at 5 o'clock a.m. in the dark kitchen
of his suburban house, 42 years old, 1985,
double-tying his Nikes. What amazes
me all over again is how fat
he has got, so bending over in his chair

in his sweatpants, he can hardly see what his
hands are doing, the fingertips
nail-bitten and bulbous, just as they were
when he was a kid. In his mind
this morning and every morning he rises
on almost no sleep, so high
it scares him, is the lovely
face of a woman, this one
he now takes out the front door

quietly, not to wake his wife
and children above his head, and there
beside his big American dealer car
and the trees untangling their leaves
from the dark, he begins to run,
fuck everybody, through the narrow street,
taking the air into his lungs as if
breathing for the first time, sending each
neat lawn, each white clapboard house behind him

and away until he is up to speed
at last with this relentless,
beautiful feeling, this terrifying
rush of joy whose name is her name
which he now murmurs, lifted into the high C
of his obsession, no mother, no brothers, no wife
and kids, no cars passing him, this oblivious man

with sweat opening at the center of his shirt, oh
my brother running too fast down the road to his death.

2 ❧

Don't think I haven't noticed it,
this thing that comes into my voice
when I talk about him,
but four years later, here's
how it is: I still find myself staring
at the puzzle of leaves outside my window,
suddenly awake in the dark just before
the time of his running and saying
"No," right out loud, seeing only then

Bob has closed the door so lightly
and walked out past the add-ons
of family room and porch which never
made the small house big enough
in some other time; that my little brother
has already lain down in his bed
after six crazy months of it
and one last, long journey of his heart
while his wife climbed on top of him

and breathed into his mouth
and his little son, God help him, beat
and beat on his chest, discovering
perhaps the slightest smile on his lips
like the smile in my dream
when I tell Bob that someone has died,
someone we knew very well, seeing at last
that the one who has died
is my smiling brother himself—

leaving me with such
fragments! A red football
he threw twenty years ago

in the K-Mart, all the way
from Sports where he couldn't breathe
for laughing to Stationery where I
saw it wobbling down from the ceiling
and caught it right in front of the clerk:
telling him I'll never go into a store

with you again, and shouting
at him from my bed with the worst
hangover of my life, "This is the last
time I ever go drinking
with you," while my crazy brother
followed my face under the covers, kissed it
with a cold beer, then lifted the bottle
high above his bobbing Adam's apple
and drained it. Loving my screams,

of course, wanting me to say I'll never
get into an automobile with you all those times
he pulled out in his big car to pass my poor,
anxious, dumb neighbor George Koehler
on a double yellow line at the same
curve, giving him the finger up through
the sun roof. That was the way
my brother was, doing seventy
and smiling that shit-eating smile,

knowing the next day I'd be right
there with him, just as he knew that afternoon
twenty years later when I opened the door
to discover him, grown skinny from all
the running—knew that when he smiled
this time, I'd be unable to say
I'll never go or get into it,
but would take the hand he held out and go along
and get more deeply than ever into it.

3

Still it was a strange moment to find my brother
suddenly there, jerking my hand—not the fat,
successful teacher and car salesman on Christmas cards
his wife had sent each year mechanically
and with much love, but this new
thin Bob with a rack of tall-boys
under his arm as if twenty years
had never happened. Except,
of course, this Bob had gray hair

and a way of going slightly
walleyed when he focused on you
so he seemed to be somewhere else
in his mind. Except he had his oldest
son with him, Patrick, the same kid
who in three months would be trying to call
Bob back from a heart attack
and who already felt something
was wrong for his father

to have driven all the way from Boston
to central Maine to see the brother
he almost never saw, the one his mother
never liked. So there, trying to talk
between the boy's quick, suspicious returns
from patting the dog outside, we were:
and there with that spacey
look in his eye, this brother
I hardly knew began to tell

his story of the small house
where the fat man with two jobs
and never enough money apologized over
and over to the wife, and the sad
acrobatics of their sex when even
her uterus resisted him, and the three

sons she had at last, whispering to them
and taking them to mass where she whispered
to her family, too Catholic after all

those years to take him in, and the whole
country-and-western breakdown of I can't
live this way, Bob spitting up blood
from the drink, Bob opening up
new rooms looking for space
in the house that grew smaller as he beat
and beat it with his hammer, nights, weekends,
year after year, walling himself into it all
over again. Until, he said, he found this

woman: and all at once, think fast,
her photograph came floating
down through the air from the same hand
that once threw the football, and he
was smiling in the old way. Except
as he bent now by my side
in the late lamplight, not quite believing
her picture himself, he was whispering still,
though by this time his son lay asleep

and my wife lay asleep, his breath
in my ear so in that family of whispers
I could hear the strain of the secret
that now bound me, the woman I'd never met
and my brother, high, exhausted, going out
to the car to bring in his strange manuscript
about our dead stepfather, and whispering,
three o'clock in the morning, as if our day had just
begun: "You're the writer. What do you think?"

4 &

So sometimes when I imagine my brother running
through the morning dark, he is thinking

about our stepfather—about all
of his fathers. Just leaving the shut lids
of clapboards behind him on his street,
just beginning to carry the woman's face far
from here, he sees the lit window
of his in-laws' bathroom drift by
above his head and they come into his mind:

she earplugged in the far room, dead
to the world, and he, the father Bob once
adopted, up alone waiting for himself to pee.
My brother wants to laugh at the poor, dopey dick
put to sleep by a million pious refusals,
then carried off to soft sheets
in the morgue of a separate room,
but instead he finds himself running faster
and weeping so, he cannot stop.

Or here is Bob tying his sneakers
in the dark of his house when the woman
will not come. He feels a slight
pain in his chest and wonders why
he is thinking about the father who left
one night for good, rising (as Bob himself
now rises) above the heads of his three
sons until he is a cigarette's high red star,
until the star winks out

and my brother, turning toward the door
in his own dark, discovers
he is not only thinking of his father,
he is his father. And of course running
toward the woman, though she's
not on this street where fathers
and children sleep, nor on the next,
nor miles and miles away, where the great
carriers of cables rise over him one

by one like ghostly icons, impossible to reach.
Is it out here one morning, running past the strip's
dead end toward these, Bob sees the stepfather
rising over him on a bucket of mud
dug from the well? Above this father
of his manuscript, twisting high in the ropes,
the crossed beams of a tripod.
Beyond him, a truck backs, lifting him
as young Bob and I stand by the well-tile

looking up. Now, half in French, he is cursing
our older brother Jim for jerking the truck.
Now he is breathing his asthmatic breath
and twisting toward Bob, who reaches terrified
across the well-hole and cannot, does not dare
to grasp his hand. Or is the stepfather still higher,
on top of the newly raised house dangling
a hook? Does Bob look up to find him on the day
three skinny kids carry a rafter so big

they cannot lift it, so big my brother, running,
feels a weight now on his chest that grows
as he goes faster past this tower
and past the next, alone with his thought
of how roofless, how homeless he is
but for this huge rafter at his chest,
and how fatherless but for this man
in the clouds, shouting and dangling
a skyhook no one of them can reach.

5 🙞

When my stepfather died in the summer
of 1985, everybody in the country
seemed to be at the movies, watching the second term
of Ronald Reagan, who'd just come to town in a blur
of flags, won the nation's heart and was romancing her
in the longest feature he'd ever made. Big business

176

was up, defense spending was up, Christa McAuliffe
was in Washington promising to take the souls
of everyone who hadn't won the Teachernaut contest up

with her. That summer in New Hampshire, meanwhile,
my stepfather got down under the same junk car
he'd owned all his life, pulled out the transmission,
and in what must have been a mixture of surprise
and recognition, watched the thing roll off
its blocks on top of him and snuff
his asthmatic breath. It hits me now
that nobody was there, any more than we were there
when my brother, shortly afterward, sat in the darkness

with the woman in his head, bent over his Nikes.
The radio in the grass beside the collapsed car
whispered a golden oldie to itself.
In the barn behind it, broken hoes
and wrong-side-up spades stood there
looking at nothing, and far off where plants
broke out of their pots and vetch twined,
the rows of twenty-five years' worth
of a failed nursery went on falling

out of perspective, collecting the dark—
the whole weedy empire lost
to the Shop-Rite bush and tree concession
off I-89, and he himself now lost
with it: the father of his stepsons' trauma,
the father of Working To Earn the Joy
That Never Comes. No more anger
about the life which, hands full right
to the end, he could not grasp and take;

no more in those dead ears the voice
of his wife saying, "You always, you never,"
the voice become his own; only
the wild, repetitious stuttering of goats

unmilked and unfed in their pen
until I myself arrived to milk and feed them,
and my brother came, and the three of us,
all that could be salvaged from the dead
habit of family, went together into that dark,

my mother in the lead saying, "What
is going to happen to me next,"
Bob close behind with the flashlight asking
"How could he have owned such a car," and I,
unable to take in how old my mother seemed,
how fat my brother had got and the death
all at the same time. Then my brother touched
the light on the old junker, deep in its tires.
Then he touched it on the matted grass

and while my mother, too bitter and tired almost
to care, told how Lloyd came over
to jack the damn thing up and pull the body out,
I saw the image of my stepfather's face,
free of its cap and floating in its hair,
eyes closed against the world of auto parts
and all the other pieces he could not
find a way to fit together, this world
which he now left to each of us.

6 ❧

I see at least one
of the family dead every day.
Walking the dog, I end up in Chicago,
where I have never been, on March 26,
1973. Beside me in the front seat
of another car sits my abandoning father,
not in the least surprised I have joined him
in this moment before he goes into the supermarket
for more beer and keels over

with his own heart attack.
Holding the gearbox in his lap
and wearing no socks, he doesn't tell me
he knew Kennedy or just had dinner
with Kissinger. In fact, you can see
from the way his hands are shaking
he doesn't have a story left,
but this doesn't matter.
I've come to tell him it's OK

he ran away from me and all
the rest of his fucked-up life—
that running from me so long and so hard
is a kind of love. What happens instead,
of course, is he turns toward the door,
opens it with his trembling hands,
and leaves me sitting there with the hard
slam of metal on metal in my ears.
It is the same when I imagine

myself getting used to the darkness
underneath my stepfather's car. Lying there
closer to him than I have ever been,
I want to say it's not important
the two of us once touched only
with our fists. I want to tell him
I know how hard it is to get life right
the first time, no second chance. Neither of us speaks.
I make out the terrible concentration on his face.

Nothing I can say to my little brother
will make any difference either,
of course, as he stands there
beside the dropped car, banging
the flashlight slowly in his hand,
the conflict he feels just setting him
into motion. Two days later
he is looking down at the closed
coffin in such a composed,

proprietary way he himself
would never guess he is making
up his mind to run. Here,
if I could, is where I would
speak to him, here as he leans down
to listen to one more secret his wife
whispers into his ear: *Brother of mine,*
it is not you under that lid,
not you who will never get out

from under the ground, go slow now.
Still composed, my brother raises his head.
Nearby in the church, my exhausted, disoriented
mother is laughing among friends she knew long ago
as if after all those years of wandering
among shrubs and trees nobody wanted,
she is being given a party. All day
the poor farm women come with cakes
and casseroles to her door.

7 ❧

All day while Bob's wife stares at their clothes
and keeps her children together on the couch
as far from harm as possible, the same
news clip of George Bush and Christa McAuliffe
in the White House with big hands
and flat heads plays on the shot TV.
For my part, I'm gofering beer
from Bob's 12-pack in the refrigerator
while he travels from dead rototiller

to failed water pump to tractor stopped
cold in the tall grass, trying to make them go.
You are not alone, I would say in the one
more night coming down. *If there is a lid to lift,*
let us lift it together. What I do

at the time, though—not knowing anything
more about engines than I ever have,
and missing the drama of my poor
brother underground trying to get out—

is pass the tools and the beer and watch
the whole evening unfold without a clue.
Now Bob stands up beside the tractor
in the growing dark, his hands
hanging there as if stunned
by all they can't do. Now he turns
toward the barn and walks as if
carrying the hands to where they can do something,
anything, and I see then it is pure rage

that takes him across the field, all
by himself though I follow, afraid for him,
past the goats whickering in their pen,
to the death car where he stops and lifts
up the old hood, folding it in half
like a bed sheet, and pops off the air
filter and snaps the antenna and kicks
and kicks the front wheel until he falls backward
and I rush to help him calling, "Bobby, Bobby,"

as I did when he pulled some crazy
stunt twenty years before. But my brother goes on
gathering the hubcap he sprang loose
and the other junk and heading for the house,
one hand free to open the door, which he does,
though I am right in his face
at this point asking him what the fuck
he is doing—pulls the gasping
door spring all the way back and dumps

the stuff on the floor. Looking around then
at those astonished faces, did I remember George Kohler,
or the clerk at the K-Mart watching the football

come out of the ceiling? Did I sense
Bob was somehow trying to free himself?
I only know that upset as I was, I almost
wanted to smile. There by my dumbfounded mother,
my French-Canadian step-aunt and uncle inched backward,
he swearing Jesus-Christ, and she crossing herself.

Beside the couch, where Bob's wife crowded
the children even farther back in their seats,
stood skinny, pony-tailed Lloyd and his family
from the garage across the road, all about to drop
their plates full of the casserole they'd just
dug into. These were the ones my drunken
brother addressed, one foot on the air filter,
his voice filling my stepfather's house: "Nobody's going
to put on my tombstone life's a bitch and then you die!"

8 ≈

Ah, Bobby, when you looked at me as if
to invite me, then left the house to run
for the first time, I should have gone with you.
What did I think I was doing staying behind
to pick up that junk, there was so much junk
already, the stacks of newspapers, the lit, lifeless
aquarium with the diver on its side
under a broken pump, the blown-out TV flipping
Christa McAuliffe up out of sight over and over.

Meanwhile, you yourself are disappearing
beyond the arc of the night light at Lloyd's garage,
thudding down the road in these incredible
fucking work boots. If I had been here
with you as I am now, I could
at least have talked you out of these.
Hearing you strain for breath already,
this out of shape, all I can think of
Bob, so help me, is your heart,

banging away at those arteries
that hardly open, and I want to scream
no again. I could have talked to you
about the stepfather you never did
escape from, or the wife you are beginning
to hate, or how your whole life suddenly
seems like one of the dead machines farther
and farther behind you in the dark. Except
that sometimes, Bob, when a car shines its

oncoming light on you moving your fists
back and forth above your stomach in this way
you learned as a kid in high school, your head
thrown all the way back, it is not rage
I see in your face, but a smile
that says you don't know whether you are
somebody's son or somebody's husband or even
in this world. In your mind, where the sun is out,
you are just meeting the woman, your secret

so perfect nobody knows it yet, not me,
not the woman, only you, gasping for air again
and again in your amazement. The wind in your mouth
is also in her hair, for after all that
lovely fumbling for the stick-shift alongside
your leg to get the brand-new convertible
out of the car lot and onto the thruway
for a test drive, she's got it up
to sixty and you are starting to feel the knot

in your groin which you call "lover's nuts,
for Christ's sake," whispering it to me at five o'clock
in the morning on your first visit to my house,
"the worst case I ever had." In that spacey eye
you are a boy again, we both are boys
again discovering love, and you add, "I don't mean it
in a dirty way," and then you tighten the laces

on your sneakers and rise with the same
crazy smile on your face to walk out the door

and run, as you do now in this darkness,
past the ghost farmhouses, past the well-lit
condos built to look like farmhouses
and into the dark again where each road sign
says nothing at all and a dim-windowed trailer
drifts far off in a field. That lost, Bob,
and the two of us also lost, you running
toward your death, I keeping you alive in my mind
though I can hardly bear the thought of your running.

9 ॐ

But how can I let go
of the two of us? Where can I lose
this memory of my brother? Just when I turn away
from his running, I find Bobby sitting down
on the floor of my apartment twenty years ago
after the appendix operation that damn near killed him,
making his absurd TV antenna. Somewhere out of view,
his professors at the teachers college
I attended and got him into are pissed off

about the tests he's missed. Out of view, my wife
and stepchildren and my desperate struggle trying
to be a father and make a home. In this memory,
just big enough for my brother and me,
he is surrounded by shirts,
and in his lap a Sears catalog is open
to the antenna section and the particular model
he is copying with coat-hangers. His
looks like a deformed dragonfly

missing one wing, which, carrying him
another hanger in a shirt, and about as drunk
as he is, I am only too happy

to provide the wire for.
What happens when my wife comes back
with the kids to find us here, and how
I deal with being so broke
all I can afford for the TV are these
drunken loops he now installs, or how,

for that matter, Bobby makes it through
his college term, the memory refuses
to say. Only that we are bringing more beers
and he is laughing his wonderful laugh
which says look how we screwed Sears,
because "Gunsmoke" is coming in.
It was this same conspiratorial joy
four years ago on my brother's second visit
to my house, another one of my brain's

favorite hits. I'm on a beer run
with Bobby, who's up from Boston in his great,
shining convertible that makes the trees shake
their red and yellow leaves down on us
as we pass like confetti. It's a beautiful day,
and on it he has come to tell me his new
secret: that he wants to get out of his marriage
to his wife, and his mother and father
and sister and brother-in-law, and the whole

death-dealing clan. I am so damned happy
he's driven all the way here to say this,
so glad I've got my brother back,
I feel like lifting the old finger
straight up just as Bobby used to, this time
to his hopeless other life. Which is when he jerks
my arm to tell me his other secret: the big
Detroit's-last-fling, smiling grille of a car
we're riding in is the one he sold—honest to Christ,

with no profit for me—to the woman. "I just wanted you
to see it," he says, "my gift to her, our home
away from home," then smiles his spacey smile
and passes two cars. Let someone else worry
what he will say if he's seen driving it, or that this
is the only automobile in the outsized fleet
he managed to sell all summer, or how he'll break
the news he's just told me to his wife. It's not
my job to worry. I'm riding with my brother.

10 ҉

But of course it was my job,
and for all I wouldn't
or didn't have time to see
about my brother traveling too fast
for both of us at the end of his life,
I can't help but feel it's still
my job. And so in the darkness
of five o'clock a.m. I sit up in bed,
thinking sometimes of my brother's hair,

of that alone. Bobby himself sits up
in his bed on his third and final visit,
propped on pillows in a small circle
of lamplight. He doesn't know I'm standing here
waiting for him to glance up
from his notebook so I can say good-night,
doesn't know that I'm astonished
by how white his hair seems in the light,
suddenly understanding in this moment

that the twenty mistaken years he's been talking about
have really happened to him. That is why
when at last he looks up—my little brother
with an old man's hair and these
clunky spectacles—I feel the catch
in my throat. "I'm writing," Bobby says,

smiling because he's so in love
with the woman and this new self
he's just beginning to know

and then he vanishes: and then I'm by myself
again with the things my brother wrote.
I seldom get them out anymore,
having them by heart, the story
of my stepfather and all the other stories
he tried, top-speed, to tell, their scribbled
sentences throwing mis-dotted i's and the loose
banners of t's behind them on their way
after his relentless thought. On one nearly

illegible page Bobby is a child
struggling with his brothers to build
his stepfather's house. "Yes, sir," Bobby says
as he's been taught to say, and lifts
his corner of the huge rafter and falls
and cannot lift it. His stepfather
stands in the sky above his head,
baiting him with a hook. On another page
the angry stepfather rises out of the earth

to dangle over a well. Recalling this day
did Bob think of how Jim, through with being cursed,
charged the truck at the tripod
and sent our stepfather unraveling down
into the mud dark? Did he remember the beating
that made Jim run to his other father
and go with him from bar to bar
while that sad man told tales of the sharpest
characters he ever met and didn't remember

the next day sober? Bobby's own story
includes only this father who twists
and calls to him over the well's depth,
holding out the hand he does not dare to take.

And now I turn in my mind's notebook to my brother's
strangest story, where he has placed himself deep
down in an open grave. Above him, the woman cries again
and again (in handwriting so taut and baggy at the same
time it's almost flying apart), What will I do?

II ∼

On the day he died,
after I woke to the ringing phone
and asked the quavering voice
too many times if it could really
mean my brother, and after I drove
my mother, my wife and our two nearby sons
in snow down into Boston, welcomed there
by the towers that walked toward us one by one
with spaces in their hands, and after we saw

on the grainy color TV of the motel room
where we dropped our bags the small, terrible
point of light far off in the sky dissolving
into smoke over and over, and the rerun
of Ronald Reagan assuring all Americans the frontier
still existed even though Christa McAuliffe
and the other Challenger astronauts never got there,
I saw the woman. Do I only imagine
that her face, blank from her tears,

resembled McAuliffe's face? All I know is
when she came out of the crowd in the hallway
at the funeral home and spoke my name, asking it
in a voice that said at once who she was, I dropped
my eyes as if I had not heard, suddenly unwilling
to believe it was Bobby she and everyone else
had gathered there for until I myself went to see
the body in the casket, which turned out to be some guy
in a suit under a crucifix folding his hands, not him

at all, but him, oh Christ, him!
And so at last I began my search
for the woman—looking for her in the hallway,
then in the church while the shut, shining
coffin was carried down the aisle by pallbearers
I did not know—feeling somehow if I could find her,
the priest whispering his prayer of death
would not be; nor the mother-in-law
with the rosary who hugged everyone,

in love with death; nor the businesslike
sister-in-law taking charge of death's last
details and arrangements; nor the tearful wife
relieved she had got Bob, who'd never joined
the church, a Catholic grave; nor even me myself,
seated with my solemn family and craning my neck
as the priest whispered, still unable to see
that my poor brother Bobby's final secret
had turned out to be the very life he could not

reach and take. For the woman did not appear,
and my brother could not, and the priest went on
talking about the Lord's obedient servant
Robert, husband and father, at peace in the house
not made with hands, and the two families drove
in snowfall afterward to receive guests in the house
with the add-ons which Bobby's own hands had made.
Snow rested on the hats of aged neighbors who came
to praise my brother for shoveling their driveways

on his last day; snow clung to the teachers' worn coats
and to the jackets of students who never stopped coming
until there was no food left for the brother-in-law
to fetch for his wife, and the spent, henpecked
father-in-law slept like the dead in his chair.
"He was such a good boy," said the mother-in-law,
hugging my mother. "I raised him to be," said my mother.

"He taught me so much at the end, said the pleased wife
through her tears, he must have known he would die."

12 ❧

Back in my brain, far back
before the three women share
their satisfactions about the dead man
in his house, there is another house
where three small boys are holding up their hands.
"See?" they say to the father, just back
from one more long trip. There are marks
from the mother's switch even between their fingers.
"See?" What does the father say? In another room

when my father has gone for good,
my mother's face is high up
in the sewing machine's light all day,
all night. Pins shine
in her mouth. I do not dare to ask her
why my father's gone. "I'll whale you,"
she seems to say. She is bringing the switch down
on my arms and on my brother's legs
like pins, like the whale's

too many teeth. "I'll be good," Bobby says, "always
and always, I'll be good," trapped in the jaws
of the whale, sick with his dread
of the whale. Forty years later,
on his last visit, my brother is still
waving his arms and screaming,
this time about his wife. "Ah! Ah! Ah!"
he says, "this is what I do when I wake up
in the night after my bad dream of being trapped

to discover that the dream is my real life."
And I say, "You can't let her do this to you, you've got
to tell her, the secret is killing you." And he says

"I'm teaching her how to do the insurances
and the taxes first, how can you expect her
to get by after I've left her," and I tell him, "Bobby,
Bobby, where the fuck is being a good boy
going to get you, she'll hate you anyway
after the divorce." And my brother stops right there

on our walk together far off in the woods
and snow where a hundred leafless
branches are giving themselves to the wind
and the coming dark. "You think I'm not going
to do it?" he says lifting his bottle to drain
the last of his beer. "You think I'm in love
with my life as a fucked-up entrepreneur selling cars
nobody wants, one of Reagan's boys?" And up
goes the bottle through the trees,

a small football with no receiver save the wide,
luminous clearing ahead of us where it falls
disappearing under snow crust. "What I want for myself,"
he says, staring after the bottle with his spacey
eye and starting to walk until I realize
he's not going to speak this time about his teaching
or the writing he's trying to do or even the woman,
but the clearing itself: "What I really want
is to build a house a million miles from the suburbs

in a place like this—Jesus, will you look at it?"
he says, and steps off the snowmobile trail, breaking
into a run. This is the moment—my brother running
and shouting on his way to a field
in the fading light—that I remember
when my mother says, "Bob was so happy that last time
he drove down from Maine—and how, "she adds, "he loved
to visit me, in his old home." Outside the window
the road to Boston widens, and the great towers come.

I think of you, Bob, heading toward the field
that vanishes as you run, and ending up in the house
of newspapers and bags of chinchilla food and ghosts
and secrets. Above your chair in a photograph,
your stepfather stands wearing the uniform of a private
in World War II. I cannot ask you to look up
at the sadness of his assurance, just a kid
on his way to teach three stepsons the "Yes sir"
he has just learned himself. We cannot talk

about the sadness in our family of motion
without thought, or get to the bottom of all
the secrets. I can only let you go on talking
about nothing in particular and smiling, perhaps
about the woman, or the crazy house you want to build,
while your mother talks back and smiles back,
and the son you brought again, Patrick, now just a week
away from the day that will change his life, peers into
the dark aquarium where the diver lies on his side.

And in the winter darkness of the day itself,
after you've left the bed you'll come back to tonight
to sleep and die in, I can do nothing but watch
you tie your sneakers. It is impossible to stop you,
though on this morning, as on the others
when you have taken the secret only I and the woman
ever knew out past your dealer car and under the snow-
laden trees, nobody tries. Upstairs your wife is dead
to the world. Far off in New Hampshire

your mother is awake, too, carrying a bag of food
to her chinchillas, obsessed with saving
her farm home. I see the poor old woman
picking her way with the same flashlight you held
in silence beside the fallen car. In another time zone
Jim is up, in the home he sought in Alaska.

I see him there, divorced, disabled, handing a beer
to some sharp character that his father,
whom he has never gotten over, would have loved.

Far away in Maine I see myself, bent over
a desk lamp among the ghosts of my own failures
as husband and stepfather, going into the world
of my poems. I haven't yet guessed how homeless
you are—how homeless we all are. And so we move,
as you now move, Bob, taking the air deep
into your lungs, running for us all. With this antenna
I've made out of my grief, bigger than the one
the two of us made long ago on a difficult night

and higher, I see you traveling past the snowbound
driveways of the old people you will shovel out
in your last eruption of energy as if trying
to release your own bound self. You are close
enough now I can hear your feet leaving the snow faster
and faster, close enough I can hear your heart,
how it opens and opens in spite of everything
it must carry as you pass your in-laws' blank
windows and your school, dark as a closed factory,

the woman in your mind, your breath hardening
to ice. It is so cold in Florida, the o-ring seals
on the Challenger's solid rocket boosters
are frozen. Nobody tries to stop the astronauts,
on their way past cameras impatient for their flight.
Far from home, McAuliffe continues toward the launch
tower, waving goodbye. And you, my brother,
though I have built the best house I can build for you
to stop at last and rest in, you go on running.

PART TWO

FIRE

I ❦

Here was my mother beside me in the car on our trip,
holding up old family photographs, and there I was,
back in the place where she took them, suddenly
and completely a boy squinting in the light
from her camera that burned my eyes and left a gray spot
drifting across the couch and chairs. Then it was night
and I lay on my pillow looking up at her teeth. "Soon

there will be brand-new ones," she said, smiling around
the old ones that looked wrong. Everything felt wrong,
my brother Bobby's legs that hurt my shoulders
as I played horsie, carrying him to the empty
wrapper of a razor blade I noticed in the corner,
all that remained of my father. Where was my father?
Why had my mother come home without her teeth?

"Every tooth gone," she said to someone on the phone
afterward, her voice far back in her mouth
as I listened, not to the old lady showing snapshots
as I drove down the highway, but to her,
the young woman I'd left behind all those years,
saying how it hurt, how she walked almost
passing out to a cab, bleeding, swallowing blood.

And where, after her promise, were the brand-new teeth?
Her with pins in her mouth where the teeth were meant
to be, sewing pant cuffs for the clothing store
day after day, her following me from couch to chair
with the fire of her switch, asking me if I would ever
do it again, me in my bed, terrified of her anger,
tasting salt from my tears. At night the music

from the gramophone in the next apartment unwound,
running down: "I don't want to set the world on fire,"
it said, "I just want to light a flame in your heart."
And I thought of my father telling me a whole city
in Germany was on fire, Hitler gone where no one
could find him, my father himself then leaving the family
and gone. So it was just me with my two brothers

and the hurt from her camera making the small
flame of light that turned to gray inside the walls
of the house, drifting across my mother's face,
eclipsing even her. Was this my mother
who leaned down to my bed months later
saying, "You're a good boy," her perfume mixed
together in my mind with bleeding and all the hurt?

In that circle of lamplight, she kissed me, on her way
to be with a new man, and when she smiled,
I saw the new teeth. "It's your stepfather," she said,
louder this time, shaking him at me in a photograph
as I turned to her, the old woman in the car on our trip
to her own mother's birthday party and family reunion,
and our long journey together into the past.

2 ॐ

My mother's photographs, by then, our first afternoon
out of New Hampshire, were everywhere—
on the dashboard, in and out of the album on her lap,
and lifted up between her fingers again and again
as my two children in the rear seat, all hot breath
and knees in my back, leaned forward trying to see.
"Who's that, right there," she asked them,

showing a small brown snapshot, which turned out
to be me as a little kid smiling on a couch.
"That's the one driving this car," she said.

"I don't see any car," said Anna.
"There is no car, dummy," said John.
"Here's your stepfather again with you three boys,
building the new house," my mother told me,

and once more the knees went into my back
as my kids looked into the vanished moment
at the four of us, one now in Alaska,
the other two dead. My mother slumped
forward in her seat belt, a large cross dangling
from her neck, putting together her photo album
and her family at the same time,

until a worn stretch of the New York Thruway thumped
rhythmically under our feet and she nodded off,
the snapshots of everyone who was not there fast
in her hands. Next day after lunch, she fell asleep
over her album right in the middle of a speech
about how much work she'd always got done
in her nursery business while her neighbors were asleep.

In the rear view mirror, my young son, hair blowing
every which-way, rolled his window all the way down
to toss two plums my mother gave him out of the car,
then all hell broke loose: the wind lifting a couple
of snapshots in the air, John trying to close his window,
telling me, "I couldn't help it, they were rotten,"
and my mother sitting straight up. "Why is it so windy

in here," she asked, blinking, her hair blowing, too.
The kids began to laugh, stifling it at the same time,
as if they would pee their pants. "Why are they laughing?"
she said, and then they were choking on laughter, and
suddenly we were all laughing, even my mother. "Here,"
she said, reaching down into one of the bags by her feet
to get more plums. "These will keep you from laughing,

two of the juiciest I have," and she was right,
they stopped laughing altogether, saying, "No, no
thank you, Grammy," and getting them anyway, together
with two ancient napkins, one from Christmas, the other
from Halloween. Then my mother handed me an old
photo of the kitchen in the new house. "I always
liked the way those cupboards came out," she said.

3 ～

"My new teeth?" my mother said, squinting up at me
and grimacing around her teeth. "Why would anybody
want to talk about that?" And when I asked
about my father as a young man, she only adjusted
her cross and said, "Left us with nothing,
thought he was a big shot"—the usual. As for the fire
that just five months before our trip destroyed each

room she waved at me and fastened into the album
on her lap, she uttered not one word. Outside
our windows in the late afternoon, leaves of corn
flew by like birds in a tropical rain forest.
Were we in Ohio? I don't recall, and she
had no idea, lost and pleased as she was,
her voice nearby and far away in the thunder

from half-open windows. "Here's your big brother Jim,"
she said, opening her palm. Surrounded by family,
Jim was a boy with a wide grin and a spreading
accordion. "Oh, here's me, pregnant with Aimee
and the new house in the background." There was green
everywhere outside the car, and inside,
under my mother's eyes, the unbelievable green

of a Kodachrome lawn in the 1950's. "That's you,
Grammy?" asked little Anna in between the seats,
looking up at her grandmother looking at the picture
of a young woman through her lopsided glasses, as if

197

it were a mirror. Her old knuckles pushed the hair back
from her face. "Yes," she said, "it's me, it's me," with a faint
sigh in her voice, and the same words she used

on the day I got out of the car in her snowbound yard
after the fire. "Anybody here?" I said. The old
ranch-style house was boarded up, and the hole
in the roof made it look like a spent volcano. "Yes,"
my mother's voice said faintly through the open door.
"It's me, it's me." Then I passed through
the curtain of daylight into that sweet darkness,

where there was nothing left of the newspapers stacked
on the tables and chairs, and no tables and chairs,
and in the whole expanse of frozen gray insulation
the fire hoses had emptied out of the ceiling, all
I could see was a stuck coat-hanger, so solitary
and oblivious in the doorway light I felt like weeping
right there. Yet in that eerie dark there was no

weeping. From another world came the voices of women,
calm and untroubled, as if they were choosing fabric
or sorting laundry in heaven, and then I made them out
in the darkness, digging in the insulation and carrying
what they'd uncovered to the one whose strangeness
as she turned a small dress under the light
from the roof hole spooks me still: my mother.

4 ⚕

Looking down at her smudged, exhausted face,
I don't think about all the fights I've had trying to drag
her off that broken-down nursery, or that we never
hug each other, I just hug her, but I can't find her
inside our hug, and suddenly she's gone to the pile
under the light of the roof hole, holding up that dress,
which she once made for my sister Aimee,

and some Kodak boxes she's salvaged, then returning
with pictures inside and outside of their frames pressed
against her breast. In the half-dark I hardly recognize
the three she shows me: Aimee wearing hand-sewn
clothes and doll pigtails, smiles a doll's fixed smile,
and though my stepfather, dressed in his World War II
uniform, juts out the familiar, defiant chin,

his eyes in the shadow of his cap seem afraid,
like his puzzled eyes in the other photo from years later,
an old man with a fire blister across his chest,
just back from the homeopathic doctor she sent him to
for his despair. "As good as new," my mother says,
waving his thin body in triumph, and draws out at last
a 1950's Christ, Charlton Heston with a woman's lips

and hair. "Tell me there's no God," she says, "if this
came through the fire and was saved," and at those words
the ladies from the Resurrection Church drop
their trowels and shovels and appear out of the dark, one
by one, to shake my hand and gather around that Christ,
so you can see saving is their life. Dazed by their joy
and the dizzying sweet smell around us,

I take the flashlight they hand me and stumble across
the insulation, past burned studs and gluey wires,
where I shine the beam into my mother's bedroom,
thinking of her anger from long ago and all the fires
she ignited in my stepfather. "Lower your britches,"
he would say, taking off his belt, already out of breath
from his asthma. The bed I once leaned on is now

coiled springs and ash, the bedroom I ran to afterward,
just craters of charcoal down through the floor.
Where are my brothers who trembled there, the fire
inside them too? Where, in the wasted museum
of her room set apart from ours, is my sister?

The framed drawings, swollen from where she erased
and erased them, trying to be perfect

for my obsessed mother, and the clothes she stitched
and unstitched have disappeared into the sweet dark.
All that is left are the closet's small blouses
and dresses my mother made for her girl, her little
doll still—and behind them, in the back,
a man with gray hair shielding his eyes: me myself
in a long mirror, holding a fire in my hand.

5 ❧

Who would have thought the high-pitched
whine I could barely hear at first was going
to be my mother behind me in that burnt-out room,
who never cried, crying? Or guessed
that she would break down all over again
on our trip after I asked her once more
about my father. "Was he really a Communist?" I said.

"I'm not going to to get into all that," she said.
"Was he, though?" "He was, and the woman
in the labor union he ran off with was. Gone to rescue
all the poor people while the four of us went hungry."
"Wouldn't your family help?" She adjusted the cross
around her neck and looked at the long, lonely row
after row of Illinois soybeans passing by

outside her window, then answered. "My mother
told me you made your bed, now lie in it, you couldn't
wait to leave." "Why couldn't you wait?" I said,
and the next thing I knew she was hanging forward
in her seat belt and weeping about my sister Aimee.
"I didn't want her to leave," my mother said
from down under her white hair, "what did I do

to make her go," while I slowed the car, and Anna
asked from the back, "What's wrong with Grammy?"
"Grammy's crying, dummy," says John. "Right, Grammy?"
My mother leaned down even more, until she was rattling
the bags at her feet as if they were the reason
she'd been hanging there all along. "Grammy's back,"
she said, sniffing, and pulled out a small dress

faded from washings and torn at the seams.
"Grammy's back." Meanwhile, I was returning in my mind
to the day after her fire, when she held the same dress up
under the light of the roof hole and brought the pictures
falling out of their frames, and wept behind me as I turned
to her in Aimee's room with my flashlight. "How can anybody
see in here?" I asked her then, ignoring her tears,

and went out to her truck in the driveway to get a hammer,
determined to unseal the darkness from that house,
as angry as I have ever been. Thumping and screeching
the plywood off room after room of scorched curtains,
books hosed into corners, and melted light switches,
I thought of the waste of family deaths:
my stepfather undoing the transmission of the junk car

that rolled off its blocks and killed him, and my brother
Bob, the jogger, running each day from the suburban life
he couldn't stand until his heart exploded. And I thought
of Jim in Alaska, where I found him years before
in his flak jacket from Vietnam with the dead soldiers
of Budweisers at his feet, tearing open a broken-down
love song on his accordion that spoke for us all.

6 ✺

So there we were, driving across the line of her home
state of Missouri, my mother bent over
her scissors clipping open the seams of that dress,
and I, angry all over again about the fire

and her decision, in spite of every objection I had,
to save the shell of that house and rebuild it.
"You'll never get the burn smell out of it, never,"

I told her, meaning more than walls or floor. "Let it go,
let the nursery go, it was done in long ago by the Shop-
Rite and K-Mart nurseries off I-89 anyway."
But she and the church ladies went on loading the junk
she'd saved into her truck with the same resolve
she had now, jerking out the old thread. "I think this
would look real nice on Aimee's youngest girl,"

she said. "Maybe she can wear it to the birthday party."
Up from the bags within bags came a spool of thread
and a needle, and for the second time, the worn envelope
containing Aimee's promise after years of living apart
in rural Virginia with her family, all born again,
to be at the reunion. "Did I show you this?"
The return address she pointed to floated in a heaven

of angel stickers. "I bet that husband is the one
who's kept her away," she said, as she always said.
"Imagine that nut claiming everybody in our
family's nuts!" She yanked the thread and cut it.
"Maybe the man is right," I said. "Well, look who got up
on the wrong side of bed this morning," she said.
High on being in the familiar, green country

that unfolded around us, high on the prospect of being
with Aimee, she was unshakable, even when we heard
the sudden, relentless arrhythm of a flat back tire.
My mother was the first one out of the car. "Look
at that mockernut tree," she said, pointing at the grove
just beyond the breakdown lane. Hump-backed,
the dress still in her hand, she gazed upward

and walked, the kids behind her, toward the high crown
among the pines. Meanwhile, I looked at the tire

weighed down by the tub on the roof-rack, then opened
the trunk, its spare down underneath an intricate puzzle
of luggage, disgusted with myself that I could've agreed
to a trip that brought me here. "It's a miracle,"
my mother said about our spot, finally returning

with the kids, who jumped into the back as I repacked.
"Imagine, parked next to the same tree that grew on our old
farm," she said. "We can't take that thing," I told her,
watching her arrange a mockernut branch across her bags
as she sat in the car. "What's wrong, Dad? This is fun,"
said John. "We're exploring America. Right, Grammy?"
"No. *Grammy's* America," Anna said back. "Dummy."

7 ❧

"Do you remember that truck?" says my mother's
baby brother Wendell on the windy night
before the reunion, no baby now, a cop
idling his squad car in the parking lot of a mall
in Springfield, where we've come to find the location
of the old family house. "Homer told me
about the night Daddy and Mama drove you kids

up here from Texas, the four of you under the tarp
of that old rig on top of everything they owned
and you hanging onto your dolls." "It was awful,"
my mother says, in between Wendell and me, "just awful.
The wind way worse than it is now, and sand stinging
your arms and face. Then leaving your home behind."
"I bet you've got a lot of fire power in that gun,"

John says through the cage behind the squad car's
front seat. "What gun?" says the face of his little sister
beside him. "You better have a lot of fire power
in a city like this," Wendell answers. "But where
was the house we had?" my mother says, upset by all

the change. "Where were the back forty acres we cleared?"
We follow Wendell's finger out the window

past the arc lights of the parking lot to the huge store
of a grocery chain. "Now the tomatoes and peas
we kids was always trying to grow up through
the tree roots are all indoors," he says. My mother
stares out the window, the reflection lighting up
her glasses. An empty can blows across parking spaces
and under a car. "I'm rebuilding my place," she says,

"it's going to be just like it was." Wendell turns
and smiles, and I suddenly see from the way
he's looking at her, my mother is his mother, too,
and the mother of the rest, back in his living room
late at night sitting with their husbands and wives,
even the oldest of them, Mae, though her mouth
is pleated around her false teeth like my mother's,

and she has the same white hair. "You was always
the talented one," Mae says to my mother.
"I remember the lovely drawings
you used to fuss over, and the doll clothes
you made, and how excited you was to of been
accepted at the state college." And Homer says,
"You kept those houses up just perfect, both of them,

I remember that. Always yelling about some mess
we made." "It was either that or get the switch
when Mama came home with Daddy
from the cotton fields," my mother tells him.
"She was a hard one back then," says Homer.
"I remember you used to lock us out of the house
down in Texas," he adds, winking at me.

"You forgot about all the sand you used to track in,
I guess," says my mother. "We'd look in the windows
and there you'd be, with the house all cleaned up
and the dolls you made the clothes for,
like some perfect other family," Homer says,
upset about it still. "Do you remember the sand storms
that come up all of a sudden and burned the skin

on your face and got in your eyes like they'd burn
out of your head?" asks Norma. "Yup," says Homer.
"And a big one starting up the same night we left there
in the truck. Clouds of dust rising in the air like
the whole damn country was on fire." "What's that sound?"
Anna asks. "It's just a siren," says Wendell,
"from a fire engine or a police car like mine. You'll get

used to them." "Can I play with your gun?" says John.
"Never mind that, you've got to get to bed," I tell him.
"Remember how Daddy cut the truck in half
after we come up here from Texas and made a tractor
out of it to farm with?" Homer asks.
"What else could he do?" my mother answers,
put out with him from before. "It was the Depression,

you did what you had to." "Remember the tornado
that lifted and turned that old house right
on its damn blocks?" asks Homer. "Bring back
the good old days," he says. Everybody laughs.
"When I get back they should have the roof
on my house and the new walls in," my mother says
out of the blue, and when Mae reaches over

to her knee and pats her, I suddenly notice,
as I notice now recalling this moment, how fragile
my mother is—and later on at our motel, when I ask her
about going off to college to meet my father,

how tired she is. "I'm too worn out to talk about that,"
she says, slumped in her chair among her bags, a branch
of dried leaves sticking out. "Tell me about it though."

She passes her knuckles slowly over her face,
emerging bitter and old. "If you must know," she says,
anger rising in her voice, "I went to college for just six
months, then I was pregnant and thumbing rides with him
all the way back East while he gave speeches about
a better life for the working man." "You're going to wake
up the kids," I say. In the silence, wind and rain press

against the windows. My mother gazes at the darkness
in the corner. "When he spoke about the forgotten
worker, all I thought about was my father," she says.
"I should have thought more about me." In the dark place
where she stares are the girl she once was, the father
I have sought, and Aimee, whom my mother and I
have both guessed by now is never going to come.

9 ⁊ⱬ

After our trip to the reunion in Missouri, when my mother
lay in the hospital with the stroke that paralyzed
her left side, I thought about the anger and destruction
I'd discovered in her past, and about my own unseeing
anger on the day I found her rebuilding the house.
Pulling into her driveway from Maine for the second
time that winter, I spotted the workmen going in

and out of the front door carrying trash bags
of insulation and charred pieces of studs and beams
to the dumpster. I slammed my car door and shouted
at her where she stood in her truck piled high
with all the stuff she'd saved. "You've got to get into
something smaller and sell this place," I said. "The only
money you'll ever have will come from the insurance

and the sale of your land—get a clue!" Replaying
that scene one more time, I see how quiet
she becomes in spite of me, loading on another burnt
chair, and how sure of what she must do.
"There are things in this world more precious
than gold," she says, far away in her eye.
And I say, "Mother, Mother, the fire was bad enough,

let's not make it any worse." "Maybe it wasn't a bad
fire, maybe God wanted to test me," she answers,
and the church ladies standing around the load
say "Yes" and "Amen," and the one in the cab
turns the worn-out truck over until it shudders
and catches. "I can't help it, I just have to,"
my mother says finally, sitting down among all

the belongings she has. Watching again the truck
that teeters slowly down the driveway toward
her neighbor's shed with the bumper sticker that says
Let Jesus Be Your Shock Absorber, and the New Hampshire
license plate's motto, Live Free Or Die, I do not see
a determined old lady with a humped back
and white hair, but instead, a scared young girl.

That long fall, propped on her pillow in her room
at the hospital, one hand laced to a bottle
that dangles from a hook above her head,
my mother has no determination left.
Sometimes when I arrive for my visits, I discover
two or three of the ladies from her church
talking to her and holding her hand, and once

I find my sister Aimee and her husband Mike,
who've driven all the way from Virginia.
Pale and fragile as ever, and still shy
of the old woman even though she lies powerless,
Aimee is holding up color photos of her family

and her house, as if this is her last chance,
and only her mother can bless what she has done.

10 ❧

I couldn't avoid thinking then of our mother
at the birthday party and family reunion,
showing the album she had brought halfway
across the country to her own mother,
the ancient woman with the lopsided wig
next to me at the head table. "This don't
taste right," her mother, my grandmother, said,

smacking small bites of the birthday cake
someone had placed in front of her. "Clean up
them plates," she said to my children,
"or you won't get none," and Mae and Homer
told her, "Shush, Granny," because my mother
was at the microphone in front of our table
starting to show her photographs page by page:

three boys helping their stepfather build a house,
she pregnant with Aimee in front of it
on the deep green lawn, the whole family around Jim
and his accordion, smiling as if with a happiness
too great to bear. Holding the album up again
and again, my mother looked down with her hot
face at Granny alone, and Granny,

not quite getting what all the fuss was for,
looked right back at her, smacking her cake.
"I don't think your mother even knows what
you're talking about," Aimee's husband Mike said
in the hospital room as my sister put the pictures away.
Under thick eyebrows, his suspicious eyes
went back to my mother's face. Now Aimee

was standing up with her bible in her trembling hands,
a cross shining at her neck, while he stood wide
and tall beside her. "The new morning will come,"
she said to my mother, helpless on the bed,
and he said it too. "Come," my mother said
out of one side of her mouth, her eyes
filling with tears. Aimee nodded, peaceful now.

"All we have to do is obey the Lord," she said.
"Amen," Mike said, frowning his thick eyebrows
together, then adding another "Amen."
"Come," said my mother, trying to lift her one
movable arm, the tears spilling down
into her hair. "That's right," Aimee said.
"For God's sake, Aimee," I said: "She means you."

Turning back to me and crying
a little herself, my sister was there
and not there. "She means Jesus," she said
and leaned forward to adjust the large cross
on my mother's chest. Then her upset,
suspicious husband turned back to stare at me
with his thick frown, there and nowhere else.

II ❧

"This will not stand," President Bush shouts
as he brings his fist down in the TV show
that recaps the Gulf War; then missiles open
in the sky above Baghdad like violent,
continuous lightning; then a general
in neat fatigues holds a pointer at a map.
"Is that Jim?" my mother asks from her bed in rehab.

My little daughter sits by her overnight bag
studying her grandmother's mouth moving
on the side of her face. "No," I say, "it's not Jim."
On the videotape that the general shows

209

there is no fire or screaming, just a small,
sudden indentation in the frame of a bombsite.
The woman in one ad is surprised how easy it is

to clean her kitchen appliances, and a family
in the next is eating bowls of cereal, then cookies
they made from the cereal. "Where's Bobby?"
my mother says. "How can you tell what she means?"
Anna asks, studying the mouth. "You have to listen
very hard," I say. "Afterward you have to think about it."
"Why does she talk like that?" she asks.

"She's very, very tired." "Where's Bobby?"
my mother asks again. She can't give up the past,
and revisiting the darkness that falls around us
one afternoon in early March, neither can I.
I lift her cold hands and rub them again
and again, then bend to take her in my arms
and hold her, remembering how she bent to me

years before in the lamplight, apart from anger
or fire or music unwinding and running down,
to kiss me. And I remember the workman
who told me he lifted and held her in her house
after the quick lightning of her stroke, her leg
and arm and face unwound, her body run down.
"Your mother was lugging in boxes and bags

of burnt things," he said on the phone
from New Hampshire, "and a bunch of old books
swollen with water from the fire hoses. I don't
understand why anybody would want to save stuff
like that." The ladies from the Resurrection Church,
understand. Arriving in the rehab room the next day,
my daughter and I find them sitting around

my mother's bed wearing scarves and work jackets
and ashes on their foreheads, explaining everything

they've done so far to fix up her house. "We brought in
all the chairs," the obese one says. "They don't smell
that bad, even without paint. And we put your lovely
picture of our Savior right at the center of one wall,
with all your family photographs around it."

12 ❧

"We even got Aimee's burnt clothes washed up," she says.
I think of my mother lying there on that Ash Wednesday
wearing ashes herself, one eye wide open, the other
a half-shut lid, and I think of the five of us
who stare back at her, waiting for her to speak:
the church women, ridiculous and moving
in their attempt to save her home,

me, wishing they could succeed, in spite of myself,
and Anna, watching my mother's mouth
to hear what she means to say, until at last
she makes her four words of longing
that have nothing to do with us or the safety
of home. "Where's Aimee?" she asks, "Where's Aimee?"
and Anna, turning to us and pleased with herself,

begins saying it, too: "Where's Aimee?" That night Anna
asks me what the gray stuff is on Grammy's forehead.
How can I tell her about my mother's need
for penitence and hope? I tell her nothing.
My mother's eyes flutter open. "Was there really
a fire that destroyed my house," she asks, her voice
as clear as it has ever been, "or did I dream it?"

In my dream of the house in the 1950's,
the Korean War is over, and it is a time
of peace and prosperity at home, just
as the President has said. The dizzying, sweet smell
in each room on this spring night comes not from fire,

but from the new floor and studs my stepfather
has nailed into place all day, exhausted now,

asleep in his chair. There are no walls between us yet.
If I were to raise my head, I might see him
under the lamp as I do now, the anger lifted
from his brow and house plans in his lap,
blue as a blue sky. But in the darkness
cast by the studs of our new room, I am asleep too,
with my brothers, Jim holding his pillow

with arms so small, it is impossible to imagine them
inside the sleeves of a flak jacket, Bob so young,
he would never think of being a runner,
even in high school. By the light of her sewing machine
my mother rests her head on one shoulder and smiles,
dreaming, perhaps, that the child swelling inside her
will be a girl. Patterns are spread around her. The new

portrait of Christ as Charlton Heston leans against
photographs on the wall behind her, ready to hang.
Watching the sleepers, he seems the only one left awake
besides me, looking on them as my mother would, if
she could open her eyes to see her family as they were,
as they must have been on this night where I
have found them, taking this picture to save them all.

PART THREE

DWELLERS IN THE HOUSE OF THE LORD

PART I

I

Inside the box she sent is bubble wrap
folded over and over around
a thick envelope, awkwardly folded,
and deeper down, wrapped
in Christmas paper with my name
on top in a blur of letters
handwritten over and over,
my younger sister Aimee's late gift,
sealed in an old plastic bag
like a secret she wants only me
to know: a silver charm bracelet,
which in the winter light of my kitchen,
dangles a palace, a running horse,
a heart with a key, and a clock.

Once, after returning from a long visit
with our mother, Aimee, married
with two daughters, hid under her bed,
keeping herself a secret. Mike searched
and called for hours before she called back
at last and he found her, discovering also
his unshakable, lifelong anger at the woman
my sister had tried to put out of her mind.

But Mike was her replacement
for my mother.

A mind has so much to keep track of:
which secrets to share,
which to guard from others,
and now, who and where anyone
is anymore. In Aimee's letter—
creased and re-creased from
her underlining and afterthoughts
in the margins—she asks me to mail
her Christmas cards for my children,
having forgotten their addresses
and their names. *They can't hear
my chattering*, she writes,
*but can read of several things
I wanted to write inside the card itself.*

The Lord loves you, she remembers
on the back, where a single heart
floats in a blank sky.

2 ❧

In the famous family photograph,
Aimee sits on the couch beside Mike
in his Navy uniform, holding his hand
and looking up at him with the defenseless
wonder she wore all through girlhood.
Eight years old, she has just asked him
to marry her. Nobody would have guessed
he would come back later to do it,
or that he would take her to live with him
north of a Navy base in rural Virginia,
his smiling, clean-shaven face now
overgrown by an unkempt, anti-social beard.

Outside the back window
of Aimee's second house

from the time they moved in,
the high, dangling chains
and gambrel stick
of a deer-slaughtering station.
In the front, open all day,
Mike's gun shop. "Obama
is going to make me rich,"
he says one night, chuckling
on the phone before handing it
to Aimee, "but I'm already
out of bullets. Everybody
down here's out of bullets."

Behind his chain-link fence, two dogs,
penned for life without names
so they won't be spoiled for hunting.

3 ༀ

One fall day in Claremont, New Hampshire,
my stepfather, who came with his family
from Quebec, Canada, took me and my brothers
to visit a Polish family in a triple-decker
apartment without enough windows to throw
off the gloom. The father produced two glasses
for drink, and at the edges of his storytelling
and gesticulation, Mike, a quiet boy my older
brother's age, emerged beside his mother,
who dragged one leg, because of a stroke
she suffered as a young woman, I later learned,
and still later, from Mike, that she never
touched him except with a switch,
yelling at him in Polish for breaking her rules,
and each week made him bring her, as if
it were his fault, the half-empty bottles of vodka
his father had hidden in the hall closet, or behind
the toilet, or under the front seat of the car.

It took only ten years for the new K–Mart Lawn
and Garden Center at the mall off route 89 to destroy
the nursery business my stepfather and my mother
had built. Afterward he lost the anger he learned
from growing up as an immigrant, and the defensive
tilt of his chin that said I'm better than you
and I'm no good at the same time. Opening himself
at last to the defeat he feared from the start,
he went back to his job on the night shift
at the same shop where his father worked
until he died. No one could reach him. Even when
my mother, grown desperate, blamed him for quitting,
he was silent, wearing the dazed look of a man
who'd awakened in the dreamlife of a stranger.

"Listen to her brag about getting food stamps,"
Mike shouts to Aimee, who's in the kitchen
while he watches a black woman
with two children in Virginia Beach on TV.
"She can't even talk right," he says.

In the presidential campaign of 2016,
two stories: on one side, the uplifting
American Story of the Immigrant,
on the other, a darker story
derived from the failures of the first,
both of them our stories.

4 ❧

For years the two of them drifted
toward each other, Mike dulled
by alcohol on submarines, Aimee

looking for a home. At age 21,
she ended up in a bathtub
in the projects of Claremont
with a French-Canadian husband
who stooped over her, starting up
a hair dryer and threatening
to toss it into the water with her.

Meanwhile, at 35, Mike spent
an entire leave and all his money
on a bar stool in Naples, Italy,
barely recalling his wife and stepchildren
back in the States. Closer now

in their drift, Mike, retired from the Navy,
wakes up in Abner, Virginia, as a Jehovah's
Witness with half his life gone to drink,
saved by Alcoholics Anonymous
and an angry God devoted to fire

and retribution. Divorced, like him,
Aimee is back home with her father,
who named her, now an old man gone silent,
and her pitiless, faultfinding mother,
more convinced than ever that the only

life left for her is her reconstructed
daughter's life. Driving to another town,
Aimee walks up four stairways of a tall
building and jumps off the roof, breaking
her ankle, her leg, and two vertebrae.

Waking in the trash of an alley, she feels
the excruciating pain of her body,
which is also the pain of still being alive.

This is the moment my fragile sister thinks of,
lying in the dark for hours under her bed
after returning to Mike from her mother's house,
with no place else on earth to hide.

5 ⁊

But before that lying in the dark,
she must lie in the zero
of a white room at the hospital,
bandaged and lost to herself.
And when at last she opens

her eyes, she finds Mike sitting
beside her, and sitting there
again the next day, just as he sat
when she was a child wishing
he would take her far away,

and after she reaches out to hold
his hand, and they go on talking
over weeks in their low, intimate way,
sometimes kissing, it becomes clear
that he will marry her and actually

take her, though the far away place
turns out to be Abner, where,
she learns in time, the anger lives,
first Mike's upset with a barking dog
next door, which he threatens to shoot

with such determination, Aimee
convinces him to start again
in another house, quieter,
she tells him, farther away, but there
she finds herself alone with his rage.

"Why," I ask my declining sister
on the phone after unwrapping
the Christmas gift she mailed,
"did you send me the charm bracelet
I gave to you when you were a girl
with a dream of horses and going off
to the palace, like Cinderella?"

"Because I kept on losing it," she says.

6 ❧

At age thirteen, after my mother, two brothers
and I moved into my stepfather's tar-papered
garage-house, I began to paint the creche scene
on its temporary picture window, guided
by the illustration on my mother's old church
program. Each afternoon as the school bus
slowed to a stop by our driveway to drop off
my two brothers and me, I saw again
the growing forms and colors of robes and canes
and donkey's ears and cross beams of a manger
transform our sad home in the snow,
no longer a place of anger, but of anticipation.
Everyone felt it, because as I painted the mantle
of Mary and the face of the Christ child
she gazed down upon, my mother was newly
pregnant. It was Aimee who lifted us up
all through the winter and into the spring
when she was born, the daughter my mother
had always wanted, and the baby sister
with braids and a smile in the framed
photograph I carried to each college dormitory
and apartment after I left my stepfather's house.

Yet this baby who smiled every time
my brothers and I held her
and spoke to her, cried herself to sleep
night after night, while our mother,
who inherited the fierce look she wore then
from her own mother, refused to hold her
so she wouldn't cry again.

Twenty-five years later, Aimee had Sophia,
named after Mike's mother, then Lena,
giving birth also to a love and hope
that went deeper than the fear she felt
for herself, though now she was afraid
for her girls. Each day as they grew up,
she lifted the invisible wet finger
of her worry, testing for currents
of inclement weather inside her house.
"'Don't bother your father,' is what I say
on the bad days," she tells me on the phone.

"He's never hit anybody," she adds,
to comfort me. "I don't think
he ever would."

In the photo Aimee mailed of her yellow
and orange beech tree in the fall,
I see for the first time the house in Abner
where she started again. Over one
of its two front doors, a sign says GUNS.

7 ⚘

This is my favorite tree—it bears leaves all
year round, Aimee wrote on the back
of the picture she sent, meaning, I understood,
how the beautiful leaves flung high above
the house had nothing to do with the troubles

inside it, like Lena's drawings of birds,
which sometimes made her cry, she told me
later in a phone call, they were so hopeful.
But on the day she called about the church
she and Lena and Sophia had found, Mike now
busy behind the kitchen door in his gun shop,
it was she who was hopeful, the bright tones
of her voice still in my mind. "It wasn't strict
and plain like Michael's church," she said,
"it was made from somebody's home, with a funny
tin hat built onto the front of it, and when
we went inside, it felt mismatched and comfortable
like a home. The worship room, you could see,
used to be two rooms," she said, "and there were
curtains on the windows beside pictures of Jesus
and the heart of Jesus with a key in it, and rows
of mixed-up wooden chairs and different-colored
plastic chairs." But what really struck my sister,
she said, was the woman who started weeping
while the preacher, Pastor Chris, was leading
the hymn about Christ's love, "weeping so loud
she said, "that Pastor Debbie went over and held her
and I started to cry, too, right in front of the kids,
because I saw that the woman without love
was me! And then," she said, "midway through
Pastor Chris's sermon about the loving mansions
in the palace of heaven, this old man stood up
and began shouting things that scared me
at first because they didn't seem to make any sense,
until I finally saw it was his need he meant,
which felt like my own need," she added, whispering it,
"and this warmth started in my chest and traveled
all the way down to my legs like thawing out,
and I stood up with the others and shouted Amen—
I couldn't help it, Wesley—Amen for the man,
and Amen for everybody around me in this church
out in nowhere, which felt like a loving mansion, too!"

Longing was what Aimee learned when she returned,
often by herself, in the months afterward, how
if she shut her eyes as Pastor Chris spoke in his sad
voice about the thirst for Christ's love, she could
almost feel the quenching on her tongue, and how
by standing with her hands out and dreaming
his sermon about the woman who touched the robe
of Jesus, she could sense it on the tips of her fingers,
as if she were no longer bound by time, but awake
in the reborn self He had promised, leaving the one
her mother and Mike had ridiculed far behind.
Sometimes, my sister said, she thought she was a little
like Jesus, each of them hiding a secret awareness
from unbelievers who meant them harm, He
through his parables about new wine skins and fruit
trees, she by telling Mike that God had helped her
find her way, and meaning the women at the local
shelter she visited on grocery days, lingering
afterward beside her favorite field to feed fresh
carrots to the horses. For as years passed,
and my nieces, one by one, left home for college,
Aimee had begun to long for her own life.

8 ~

Being bad, my mother learned
from her own church-going mother
in the Ozarks, was not trying hard enough
to stop being who you were. Being yourself
was what you got slapped for. Yet

when she was seventeen, she, too,
longed to be herself. "I can't wait
to get rid of this family's name,"
my uncle, a boy then, heard her say
in the shack where she lived with her brothers

and sisters. Then she married, had a child,
and headed for New England. Sitting
on a battered suitcase and nursing
my older brother while my father
thumbed rides for the three of them

across the country to a job his cousin
had promised, my mother never guessed
that her longing had just begun.
Four years later, she'd given birth
to three sons and lived in the projects

of Springfield, Vermont, where my father,
moving on, had abandoned her—
she, an immigrant in her own right,
with an accent her Yankee neighbors,
poor like her, strained to understand.

In the late-night quiet when Aimee
began babysitting to pay
for her escape, did she ever think
about the young woman our mother was
before turning into her own mother,

the woman who couldn't wait
to be free, too? Did she remember
her dazed, unfulfilled father at the end
of his life, as I do now, or consider
the longing of the absent fathers

who had left their homes to commute
to city jobs miles away, or the single
mothers doing double shifts at Walmart
or Family Dollar for the children
they so seldom saw? Sitting alone

beside a lamp on the worn sofa
where I imagine her, she doesn't think
of those others at all, only
about the earnings she tallies
in her secret notebook. Yet

on this night in my mind, my little sister,
alone and anonymous in America,
dreams for them all.

PART II

I ✦

I don't know exactly how Mike responds when
he sees Trump for the first time on TV,
but I know Mike. How he might laugh at first
at the ridiculous fake hair, then, just before
clicking to a cop show, get interested
in the way Trump keeps calling the runty
guy from Florida "Little Marco" with a sneer,
and makes them all seem little, especially
the moderators sitting at their desk like teachers
with trick questions: why would Mexico pay
for your border wall to keep Mexicans out,
or what about race relations, their big issue,
while the country goes to hell. In a moment like
watching the bored, disgusted face of Trump
as he turns to take on the moderators, too,
Mike discovers what he's always known:
it's the bullshit rules and the people in charge
who make them up that have been holding him
and the whole damn country back. Now
when he searches on the television for Trump
and finds him wearing a cap over the shock
of orange hair that ignited the anger
he's carried since childhood, he misses it.

But I also know another Mike. Arriving without
family at our camp in Maine for an overnight
after visiting his immigrant relatives in Claremont,
this Mike offers us a jar of his homemade Polish
jam and a larger one of preserved fish. Lacking
his rifle, he is awed by the moose we see foraging
across the pond, and in the twilight that gathers
around our screen porch, he tells us about my sister's
cat, how it can't get enough of her and follows her all
over the house for the chance to lie in her lap.
In this way, having long since submerged the feeling
life that confuses him, Mike confesses his love.

I, too, am confused. I reach out
to the Mike who calls me
Buddy, the Navy name
for friend, and in every secret
phone call, I reach out also
to my sister, bereft and alone.

2 ⚝

In the summer of 2016, when Donald Trump
appears like a god from clouds of vapor
at his party's convention, Aimee disappears.
Just behind Mike in my mind, as he carries
his hunting rifle into the house and calls
her name, I hear how he senses she's gone
and at the same time denies he senses it, checking
the empty rooms one by one: the kitchen, where
he's sometimes found her under the clock,
staring out the window as if she's forgotten
her hands in the dishwater; the living room
with its still rocker where he's seen her whispering

words he cannot hear to her cat; and finally
the bedroom, where again he says her name,
more to himself, not daring to kneel and lift
the bedspread, as he did long ago, and discover
this time a dark vacancy, like the one that now
opens inside him as he spots the note on her pillow.
In the silence that begins while he lays down
his gun and finds my sister's silent, handwritten
name beneath her reasons for leaving him,
the accusing voice of his mother, which he's spent
a lifetime pushing away, also begins.

3 🙢

One time Michael left the kitchen door open
to the gun shop, Aimee told me,
and a customer was mocking Hillary Clinton
as the ugliest grandmother he'd ever seen.
Her daughter was even uglier, another said.
A third explained why Hillary was a bitch.

When Trump says Crooked Hillary
has accused him of disrespecting women,
the men at the rally stand and chant, Lock her up!
"Nobody respects women more than me,"
Trump shouts back to them. "Greatest person ever
was my mother," he says. "Believe me, the greatest."

What the solo demonstrator at a different
rally actually wants is his mother's love,
Trump insists, over and over. "Go back
to Mommy," he repeats with an anger

so personal he seems to be battling
with himself. "Little baby, I can't stand

to look at you," he says, then flips
his hand and turns away, as if he

is the one he has put on punishment.
"Get him out! Get him of out my sight!"
The men in front with bright red
Trump caps lift their fists and cheer.

For who would question the toughness
of a man with his chin thrust out?

4 ❧

"The illegals are taking our jobs," Trump says
on the campaign trail in Richmond. "They're
taking everything, including our money.
This is not going to happen anymore."
Build the wall, the audience chants, *build the wall!*

My sister Aimee does not understand politics.
All she thinks about as she starts down the road
she's known for twenty years and sees
the Trump signs is Mike erupting at the blacks
on TV, and the hatred in the gun shop,
and the blessed lightness she feels as she sends
it all, sign by sign, into her rearview mirror.
Beside her in my mind, holding an imaginary cat crate
as she drives toward freedom, I feel the lightness
too, though I worry about the desperation
of the stained double-wide and ruined cape
we pass, and the backyard with bedsprings
and refrigerators and a Confederate flag. Not Aimee.
When I glance over at her, she stares straight
ahead, only turning to look at the broad
green field she loves, where one of the horses
seems to run with us, for after her long struggle
she's living the dream she's dreamed for years.

Never mind the closed knitting factory we approach,
then send behind us, and the big box stores
that replaced Main Street, and the high, indifferent
clock of the Bank of America. My sister is lowering
the windows and singing the old, loving hymn
about being lost and found that we once
learned in our mother's church. And I, the worrier,
the man of little faith, I'm singing it, too.

5 ⁊ℳ

But after Aimee leaves Mike all by himself
with his guns, I cannot stop my worry.
And on the evening of the election, when Trump
sweeps the towns of the Abner area and the Polish
and French neighborhoods of Claremont,
New Hampshire, going on to become President
of the United States, she seems more distant
and fragile than ever. "Please be careful, Baby Sister,"
I tell her on the phone. "Anything can happen."
Yet Aimee wants to talk about all the new people
in the church, her home away from home,
"so many, Pastor Chris preaches three times
on Sundays," she says, "and I teach two
new sessions of Sunday school. I love
being with their children," she says. "But where
do all these people come from? Poor ones,
and needy ones, I can tell by the look in their eyes!"

Awake all night, anxious for Aimee
and for the future of my country, I remember
an old photograph with a deckled edge
and take it from its cubbyhole in my roll-top
desk: me at age fourteen standing outside
the trouble of our home in Claremont
with Aimee as an infant on my shoulders,
the shadow of my older brother on the lawn

as he snaps the picture. In the half-dark
of my study in Maine, far to the north
of her secret apartment, I put the photo
in my printer to scan it for her. Seeing it again
on my computer screen, I can still feel
Aimee's trusting fingers clasp my ears
while I hold her tiny feet in my hands,
as uplifted as she is. *Us against the world,*
I write, then click and send. Up late herself,
she emails back, *Forever, you and me!*

Did Mike find the cat, or did the cat
find him, coming to the woodpile twice,
then peering through the wet dots
that gathered on the kitchen window
while Mike looked back at his green
eyes and wet, flattened ears. "You couldn't
leave him out in the rain," he told Sophia
when she called to check on him.
"And you could guess by looking at him
he was hungry, so I gave him some leftover
cat food," Mike said, not mentioning who
had originally bought the food, or that this
was a tuxedo cat like Aimee's. Sophia
said nothing, just listened to her father
remember each detail of her mother's cat,
now gone, as he told how the two of them
were different, the new cat with a long
white sock and a short white sock
on its back legs, and playful, too,
a word Sophia had never heard him use.
"Dad was just sitting on the couch watching
his cat stretch out on the rug by his feet
calling it my buddy," she told me,
"when he suddenly began to tear up,
which shocked me, because it was the first
time I'd seen him cry. But I got used to it,"
she said. "Back then, he cried all the time."

The fourth campus of the megachurch, where
Pastor Chris moved his congregation that winter,
was so big Aimee sometimes felt lost there,
but how else could you bring together so many
people, she said, which was the main point,
after all, not how she felt. And she liked how
the whole staff, from the women who greeted you
at the door to the men who helped the children
and the disabled ones to their seats, never seemed
to stop smiling. "They even have an overflow room,"
she said, "where the organ music is piped in
and the late-comers can have coffee and donuts
while they watch the service on a big TV, while
the other people watch it on the massive TV
in the worship auditorium." Aimee still couldn't
get over seeing Pastor Chris's face blown up
on the screen like that—the same person she knew
from before, yet with a close haircut and a new suit,
plus, looking like he was trying to adjust
to the whole thing himself, the way he kept saying
Amen and Praise God too much, or walking
from the stage to the podium while he was giving
his sermon to check his notes. "Or maybe it was all
me again," she said, "thinking of him as this small
man I saw from the back pacing back and forth
trying to remember his lines, and at the same time
this big authority on the screen saying them—
or what was worse, thinking of myself in the audience
with the camera running, like I was part of a show."

On the Sunday Mike came out of the audience
of the megachurch in his work pants and suspenders
and approached the podium, Pastor Chris
must have been just starting his sermon about how
Christ wants us to win in our lives with the five keys

to material happiness. When I visit the church website
after Aimee tells me about the sermon and click
just above the link with the cross for donations
honoring all credit cards, I watch Pastor Chris
preach the sermon in his slow, sorrowful voice.
But there is no trace on the video of Mike, whose face
on the big church monitor that morning surprised
my sister so much she called from the church
parking lot on her cell phone to tell me about it.
"All of a sudden Michael was up there on the screen
talking to Pastor Chris," she said, "and I could tell
from the red around his eyes he'd been crying, also
that it was all about me, but nobody else seemed
to care, all the ushers wanted to do was to get him
out of the way of the camera shot. Michael
didn't even know what was going on," she said,
"when they turned him around and guided him out
the door. Pastor Chris just went right on preaching,"
she said, now crying a little herself, "so I stood up
and left, too. What kind of a church is that?"

Two days later, when I tell her that Mike
has been erased from the official church video
and she goes online to see, I also show her the link
on the homepage, beside the photograph
of whites, blacks and Latinos standing together
in New Fellowship: a prayer of blessing
and support for President Donald J. Trump.

7 ❧

It was clear by then she wouldn't go back
to the megachurch. The bad news,
for me, was she went back to Mike. Again

and again, I imagined her on the long nights
she'd spent babysitting, accompanied
only by her dream of elsewhere,

231

or rode beside her, just the two of us,
past the Trump signs, as she escaped
from her old life. Where was my little sister?

Who was she? "Aimee, Aimee," I said
to her. "All this time I thought
you wanted your freedom!" But Aimee,

not so little, said, "Freedom isn't about
galloping off into the clouds, Wesley.
It's the chance to make your own choice."

8 ⁊

On his first days in office, Donald Trump
showed off the words of his executive
orders against Muslims and Mexicans
and healthcare for the cameras
like Vanna White on a game show.

At his winter White House, a golf course
in Florida, he sold face-time
for $200,000. "I can act more presidential,"
he said, "than any president except
the late, great Abraham Lincoln."

Meanwhile, mysteriously, Aimee began to forget.
In the spring, when we went back
to calling each other, she sometimes struggled
with words, and by the fall she was forgetting
whole conversations. Driving to meet Sophia
and take a memory test at the V.A. hospital,
she forgot the way and ended up at twilight
in a parking lot with two off-duty actors
in Williamsburg, outside of the Essence

of America masquerade party, hosted
by Presidents George Washington
and Thomas Jefferson. "For hours we didn't
know where in the world she was," Sophia said,
and I said how glad I was that her mother
had been found at last. But where in the world was I?

In that bleak time of lies and pretending
and grief, I had at least the six words
that Mike, then just back with Aimee, said
when he called me up out of the blue,
awkward, embarrassed, and determined:
I've behaved like a real asshole. In a dark time,
I had this rough, unpredicted truth.

PART III

I 🙞

Pick's Disease. Pick's Disease is an
irreversible form of dementia which

can occur in people as young as 20.
Symptoms. Symptoms include reduced

writing and reading skills. Diminished
social skills. Shrinking vocabulary.

Slowed movement. Accelerated
memory loss.

Yet what is my sister, I ask myself
on the winter morning when I receive
the Christmas cards with blank

envelopes for my children,
whom she loves, though she can't
remember their names—what is she

but a soldier against losses?
What has she ever been, putting
her own broken body back together

as a girl, then repairing her broken
heart, over and over, but a master
of trying again, mending,

as her mother, the seamstress,
once mended after my father left,
night after night, to hold herself

and her family together—
Aimee more her mother's daughter
than she ever understood?

2 🙞

And so, on New Year's Day 2018, just before
my trip to be with her, I sit in my Maine
kitchen unwrapping her late Christmas present,
the charm bracelet she's sent to me
for my safe-keeping, gradually understanding
the challenge of her gift. For all the silver
charms I unseal and lift out of the plastic
bag where they have been stored—
palace, running horse, key, and clock—
have gone dull, except for the rounded
form of the heart, which shines as I turn it
in the light. I do not know how many times
my sister, caught in lovelessness,
took it between her fingers and thumb
to rub it and make a wish against

the odds, only that the force of her hope
has outlasted the failure of metal and wishes.

3 ~

"Dad's first cat, the one that came to the woodpile,
is Pedro," says my niece Sophia as she drives us
out of the airport. "Lena named him because
the way he sometimes holds his head to one side
with his ears down flat reminded her of a sombrero.
The second cat, which Dad picked out so Pedro
could have a friend, is Baba, his shelter name,
a big old tabby cat. The other two love Baba,"
she says. "Wherever he is, they want to be,
and Dad, too. It's like the damn cat owns the place."

Meanwhile, having left her three-year old son
behind with her husband in Norfolk, she heads
toward the place she means with steadiness
and efficiency, untangling the knots of thruway
that lead us north on 17 to Aimee's sad town
which seems, when we arrive there, motionless
by contrast, its deserted main street now a one-way
to the big box stores at the outskirts, its old brick
knitting factory now rows of vacant windows.
Then, by some turn I haven't followed,
we're twisting through the snowy, hilly roads
of Sophia's girlhood, with trucks in the driveways
we pass and old cars marooned in the yards,
until she swings in behind Mike's pickup
and we're suddenly in her parents' yard.
"Like I mentioned," Sophia says, gesturing toward
the clutter on the porch, "things have slipped
a little since you came a few years back, outside
the house and inside, what with Mom and all."
Then I see Aimee, standing by herself
in a cap and overcoat under the high, leaf-filled

branches of her favorite tree, a study
in winter and faithfulness, waiting, like me,
after all these months of her struggle, to be held.

It was this holding and being held
after her waiting, this looking into her eyes
to find the sister I had always known,
that began to restore me. Walking with her
behind Mike as he carried my suitcase
through that house of forgetting,
past her dusty summer shoes in the hall,
and the living room chairs with yesterday's
sweater on top of the day before's shirt,
and the forgotten Christmas wrapping
and stack of mail on the kitchen table,
I thought about the sorrow of what my sister
had lost and went on losing, but most of all,
about the small miracle of her constancy.

That night after Lena arrived from her work week
at the craft brewery in Newport News, and my nieces
and I sat up to talk, I also thought about Mike,
the husband Aimee chose twice, how even
with the stress of her illness, his face had softened,
and how quick, behind his ragged beard, he was
to smile. Sophia thought one reason was he got rid
of the gun shop to take care of her mother.
"He's always had a soft side, anyway," she says.
Lena nods. "But more now. He's changed."
A cat person like Sophia, she insists
it's because of the cats. "They gave him,"
she says, "the permission to feel."

4 ⁊

Aimee is not the only one who forgets. The clothes
in the living room and the old mail in the kitchen

belong to Mike, too. Checking her pills, then
rechecking them as he puts them beside the lunch
he's prepared for her, he confesses that his forgetter
works much better than his rememberer. Yet
he remembers to bring out his box of Polish
memorabilia, which he wants to show me, he says,
because I'm family—old folk dolls passed down
to him, a silver eagle medallion, a bronze
military medal awarded to his great grandfather
on his mother's side, and then, from an old envelope,
a picture of his great grandfather himself, in uniform,
with the medal around his neck. "That was before
they found out he was a Jew and took him away,"
Mike says, "before his children and their kids
fled Poland for the United States." Then he hands me
a photograph of two I recognize: his mother and him
in their home in Claremont after her stroke.
"Whenever she made blackberry or blueberry jam,
I was the one who picked the berries," he says.
"And when she put up her jam or her beet relish
I thumbed in the rubber seals and turned
the lids down on the jars. I was always her right
hand," he says, pleased with himself, pleased
to remember himself with her. "I was her doer."

I do not recognize Mike's father in his photograph,
he is so young, standing on a lawn with a smile
in an academic robe. "When he went looking for a job,
he was turned away because he was a Polish immigrant
and a Catholic," Mike says. "Poor me! Poor me!"
he chants, mocking the black protesters against social
inequality. "Nobody ever demonstrated for him."

"I get your point, Mike," I tell him, passing
the photo back. "His situation was not so much
different from theirs. But on the other hand,
their situation is not so much different from his."

Looking down at his father, Mike does not hear me.
This man who has confessed to me his failings
of the heart, who owns that he is part Jewish,
who has welcomed lost cats with strange-sounding
names into his home, is so close to understanding,
yet does not understand. But we are talking.

At twilight in Williamsburg, two actors, black men,
walk toward their cars with their costumes
tucked away in backpacks, the same two
who discover my sister Aimee wandering alone
in the parking lot. "Who are you?" they ask her.
"Are you lost?" But Aimee keeps asking them
who they are, as if all three of them are lost.
This is the odd scene still in my mind months
after Sophia has described it, Aimee adrift beyond
safety, and the two men released from their play
as black slaves, now set free in America.

5 �☙

Given Mike's early trouble with alcohol, he allows
none in the house, but when he and Aimee go to bed,
and what my nieces and I call the night shift begins,
out comes Sophia's cooler with its contraband:
craft beers Lena has brought from Newport News,
and for the moment, Lena is not the graduate
of an art school trying to pay her bills, and Sophia
is not a computer programmer, and I'm not even
their uncle, because we are all in it together
as returning conspirators. Besides, I now see them
as the granddaughters of a Jewish woman who escaped
with her parents from Polish oppression. "You look
a little like your grandmother," I tell Sophia,
and though it's old news, I can't help mentioning
Lena's dark skin, which everyone in the family links

238

to her great grandmother on my stepfather's side,
the Native Canadian from Quebec. Lena, surrounded
by cats on the couch, sets her beer down, stands,
and pirouettes. "I am a woman of the world," she says.

6 ⁊

It's hard to tell what Aimee knows and doesn't
know sometimes, looking at you with her eyes
wide open yet speaking as if from a dream,

here, and not here, as she soon will be when we
remember her. Still she is with us, and like the rest
of us, changing every day. When I give her a hug

after she and Lena and I return from our walk,
and she surprises us by calling me Daddy as if I
were her long dead father, has she lost her memory

of me or found a new connection, suddenly aware
that the love she feels is not limited to a single name
or even to the present, but exists in a time

unknown to us, where it all makes perfect sense?
Perhaps when she sits on the couch beside Mike
looking down too long at the cat she holds lovingly

in her lap, or the face of her grandson on the iPad
Sophia hands her, smiling at him with surprise
and joy, she knows more than we think about how

time goes on forgetting her month by month,
and she only wants to dwell in the moments
that move her most. Taught by experience to live

in the world of in-between waiting for the moments
we wish for to happen, we wouldn't really know
if she's letting herself go a little each day to live simply

by touching and holding—by love, the very thing
which, without our quite knowing, she has called us to
all her life, and why each one of us has come.

7 ∼

Far in the back of the shelf above the hallway
coat rack, I spot among the other forgotten
hats the unmistakable red of a Trump cap.
I draw it out and uncrumple its message, a call
to arms against all outsiders. Make America
Great Again, it says to the wall, where I return it.

At 35,000 feet, Hillary Clinton is on her way
to a talk show in England to promote
her new book about the 2016 presidential
election. High above other clouds, Donald Trump
flies to a speech at a rally in Florida, one more
performance by the damaged maestro
of nobody loves me enough, so seductive
in his aggrievement that his anger and hatred
and longing become their own.

Here on the ground, Sophia is serving supper:
polenta with chicken and vegetables, made special,
she says, from her grandmother's recipe. "Dad
used to make it," she says. I think of Mike, the doer,
stirring polenta for his disabled mother as I settle
into my chair on this, the last evening of my visit.
"Why don't you do the mumbles?" Mike asks, taking
my hand, and, watching him, Aimee takes the other,
joined by Sophia and Lena, and suddenly they're all
bowing their heads, as if I, a practicing disbeliever,
have something to say. "Dear Lord," I begin

from old habit, closing my eyes, and in that dark
find the prayer that rests on my tongue, for us,
and for the refugees who have come before us
from Poland, and French Canada, and the wilds
of the Ozarks, in the arc of the hope of belonging.

8 ❧

Taped to the refrigerator in my sister's house
is a seasonal card that quotes the Bible's account
of Christmas. After supper and one last session
with my nieces on the night shift before I go home,
I find the card there once more in the darkened
kitchen, moved by the lopsided heart Aimee has drawn
beside its words about the wise men offering
their gifts at Christ's manger. There is no mention
of the angel who arrives soon afterward to insist
that Christ must leave, which makes this story,
I see now as I end my own story, incomplete.
For we are all born into exile, saved only by the homes
we dream, and the love that we may find there.

LATE WONDERS: NEW POEMS

THE EXIT

For days the earth has turned back
to the spreading wildfires of California
and Oregon and Washington
in its rotation, carrying vast clouds

of smoke all the way to our sunsets
in Maine. Tonight as I drive home,
an ambulance comes out of the darkened
twilight and flies past, warning everyone
it can reach with its siren of the crisis

waiting just around the corner:
cars strewn across the road among
the flashing red and yellow lights
of another ambulance, and the whirling

blue lights of local and state police,
and the lime-green rescue vests
of the Jakes called in to put out the fire.
"Bad visibility" is the phrase
the flagger uses to explain the accident

caused by the greater accident.
Then he flips his sign from Stop to Slow
and waves me and the others toward
the arrows, as if there were an exit.

THE TALLY

Those of us who warned
about the growing tally.
Those of us who called it a plot.
Those who attended church in protest
until some of them could not.
Those of us who worked

remotely from their homes,
those of us who couldn't.
Those who wanted to work,
or couldn't work at all,
or didn't have a home.
Some of us who refused
to fund the jobless
so they would get a job.
One of us who blamed
the governors and wouldn't
fund their states. One of us
who promised cures
that never came, and left
the microphone to someone else
and walked away. Those
who wouldn't wear a mask
because they loved their freedom,
those who marched for others
who weren't free. Those who said
they couldn't breathe
in the hospitals, and said it
in the streets. The many living
at a distance, the many others
who got exposed. The few
who risked their lives for patients
in the ER, up close.
The daily tally that continued.
The families struggling
to cope. The surge
in the white rooms of zero,
and empathy, and hope.

THE ARRANGEMENT

The sky and pines, and the blue
and green waves that shift
their reflection on the surface

of my pond had made
an arrangement with me,
which was to preserve the peace

while I made poems by myself,
apart from the trouble of the world,
but earlier that morning,

a mother moose wandered
down to the nearby shore to bathe
her shoulder, which had been hit

by some vehicle that she was no
match for. When I started out
at the camp to my cabin

on the water, she was still
leaning into the pond, though now
collapsed and dead. What happened

to the yearling I'd watched
her teach all spring to forage
and swim, I discovered

in the twilight, paddling past
the inlet where they'd spent
so much time together. No way

I could tell him how I felt,
and he wouldn't have been interested
anyway, seeing I wasn't

his mother. All he wanted now
was to stand and stare at me
in the half-light with his ghost

stare, and the next day,
as I started out
for my cabin, to be gone.

THE HOLDOUT

My friend Barbara, age 94, is out of patience
with her body, in particular, her bandaged foot
that stumbled over the threshold, and now,
she says, while describing her plans to renovate
her house for her grandson and his family,
her damn thumb's decided not to work. For Barb,

even death has become an annoyance. I wish
I would hurry up and die, she says in her excitement
about the house project, so the family could get
started with it. After dessert at Will and Betty's,
I tell her story, which makes us feel our own aging
isn't all that bad. Diane rolls her eyes about her fake

shoulder joint that sets off alarms at the airport,
and Betty laughs out loud when I tease her
about getting to second base with the young
physical therapist who massages her knees. But that's
not the reason Will doesn't smile. He's thinking about
the friend he had lunch with yesterday, a nice guy,

three years into retirement, Will explains, and he's got
Parkinson's so bad that when he watches you speak,
his head swings back and forth as if your mouth
is some book he's reading line by line. "So he's
watching, Will says, and suddenly this confusion
comes over his face, and I realize he's trying

to figure out who the hell he's listening to." That
anecdote, you can imagine, puts quite a damper
on our after-dinner mood, not that this stops Will,

even in the kitchen, where, as Diane and I are about
to go, he recalls that the very same expression
his friend wore used to come over his mother's face

when she got old, and then remembers his father
wasting away to bones, though if he'd only gotten
a routine checkup, he could still be alive right now—
not the now of this moment when you're reading
my poem, but back then when my friend Will, always
prone to worry, talked about death in the stove light

of his darkened kitchen, while Betty begged him
to change the subject, for God's sake, before
our company goes home. Now, it's several years
after Will—I tell you this in sorrow—fell mortally ill
himself and died, and the one thing I wanted
to remember for you about him is how on that night,

while the rest of us went on with our small-talk, humor
and distraction, Will kept warning anyone who might
listen to pay attention to time, which doesn't care
for amusement, telling his stories that aren't so funny.

LAST WORDS

I don't feel like who I am.
My pants don't even match my shirt.
I never wear my hair like this.
It feels like my legs have turned to sand.

My pants don't even match my shirt.
My roommate doesn't make any sense.
It feels like my legs have turned to sand.
I have a headache in my hand.

My roommate doesn't make any sense.
Tomorrow, my son is taking me home.
I have a headache in my hand.
The doctor won't tell me what he's going to tell me.

Tomorrow, my son is taking me home.
You can call all day here and nobody comes.
The doctor won't tell me what he's going to tell me.
There's a little cyclone in my brain.

You can call all day here and nobody comes.
I never wear my hair like this.
There's a little cyclone in my brain.
I don't feel like who I am.

LATE WONDERS

I

Every unheeded warning
Ed gave his father in outrage
was borne out in the end:
the kangaroo mice outside
the retirement home in Florida
settled in and multiplied, rising
from so many nests in the front yard
when his father appeared
for twilight feedings
that a wildlife specialist
had to remove not only the rodents,
but the landscaped bushes
from which they emerged.
Yet on this night when Ed
tells me the story of his father,
who'd spent his worklife
in the loneliness of an office, now
walking among the multitudes of mice

as he reached into a bowl
to offer them a special mixture
of peanuts and breakfast cereal,
calling the favorites by name, he laughs,
and his eyes shine with wonder.

2 ᔰ

Oddly, it was their flawed
conversations the old man
missed most, a wisp
of her white hair

loosened beside her face
as she looked to him
across the table at breakfast
or dinner for the word

or thought that had lifted
by surprise from her tongue
as if he were the only
one who could save her

from the loss of it,
not a cruel absence
as he looked back,
but something in her dear

blue eyes he wanted
to know and be with
as he helped her find
what she meant to say,

her stammering
the fullest
eloquence.

Set apart, forgotten, in Diane's figurine
cabinet, a multiplicity of terriers
she once collected sit or stand
inside the glass, each lifted paw

or cocked head chosen by grief's
recognition of a single lost terrier,
each not enough of the dog until the next
and the next, and today three dozen

crowd together staring out of their room
in the back room as if her longing
had become their longing, though if anyone
should open the door for them, they'd turn

passionless and still. Death's like that. Life's
in the sunlit kitchen, where other miniatures –
a windup cat, a bird on a wand, a fish
with streaming feathers—lie upside-down

or sideways on the floor. Meanwhile,
her new tuxedo kitten watches her search
with a poker under the wood stove
for its favorite, a green mouse with a long,

coiled tail. Now, the kitten insists
with nearly black eyes, in a voice
that's twice as big as itself. Now.

AS IF THE IRISES

As if, when she fell asleep and dreamed at the hospital,
my mother Ruth searched a field in the Ozarks
for signs of her childhood home and found
the irises, which in the distance resembled butterflies

or small blue and white and yellow birds
floating above the open space in the grass. As if
it wasn't them at all because there were too many
for the patch her mother had planted by the front door,
though what else could they be? As if when she walked

closer to find it was them, now growing across
the yard and well beyond, the old house,
which she once couldn't wait to leave,
was there too, as if it had been waiting all

this time for her to bring it back, its scuffed steps
rising up to the front door with the swollen screen,
and above them, the upstairs window slanting
under the eaves where the girls slept,
separated from the boys by a cardboard wall.

As if when Ruth bent her face down to the irises
and inhaled their sweetness, she became
her mother, not the impatient, fearsome woman
who switched her, but the one who bent down

every spring to smell them and gather a whole
armful, all colors, then set their astonishing beauty
down in a glass jar on the worn-out kitchen table
with a bang that might have broken it, but didn't,
as if to say there was something in this world

besides the nothing in the house, which made it
more than you thought you had. As if it wasn't
the house my mother had come here for at all,
her siblings withering away or dead, and even

her husband and her youngest son now dead,
but these calm, lovely flowers doing what
they were meant to do, which was to come back

in the springtime and multiply their beauty.
As if she didn't feel the old, excruciating pain

in her knees, bone on bone, when she went down
to be among the irises, caught up in the invitation
of their buds, like small fists just opening,
to put aside your pent-up conflicts and your work day

that went on and on, exactly as her mother did
when she stayed up in the dark with her sewing,
the iris blossoms now dangling around my mother's face
like the delicate ruffles of the church dresses
her mother made from disused blouses. As if

the church had given her mother a reason to spend
whole nights in the pleasure of being free from the very
children she sewed the dresses for, obsessed
with stitching the cut-up pieces together in a new way,

like Ruth herself after her daily drudgery
at her husband's nursery, sewing dresses and bonnets
and scarves all night for her daughter, who left home
early, just as her sons and she herself did. As if the guilt
she sometimes felt about her children had no place

in this endless garden, where now she was beginning
to pick her own armful of irises, white and yellow
for all the homemade dresses, assembling
her selections with the hands of the girl she was

when her mother taught her to sew, as if
choosing her, the oldest, for the secret of the nighttime.
As if her angry father was choosing her, too,
teaching her to play the autoharp for the nights
when neighbors came in their field clothes to dance

with the rugs rolled back, like the full-blooming
petals of the dark blue iris she now selected.

As if when her father held his fiddle to his cheek
with his eyes closed and played, he left his own song

behind for her, along with his hands that wagged the bow
and jumped all over the neck, and the farming life
he was never cut out for, and the deep blue-black
of his depressions. As if the joy my mother felt
as she kept up with him with her chords, stomping

her shoeless foot, was still there in her leg
when she opened her eyes at last, though lying in her bed
with tears of happiness on her cheeks, she could not
move her leg. As if, holding the irises she had gathered

fast to her breast while the next day slowly came
through her hospital window, she had all
she needed of the music and dresses and scarves
and centerpieces and painted mirrors that helped her
to bear her life. As if she would always hold them.

THE BLINKING CHILD

I remember the secret places, the hallway
with its fancy banister left from when the tenement
was a house, and the cellar under the apartment,
where I kept the stray cat I wasn't supposed
to have on account of my stepfather's asthma.
But he was all black with green eyes, and when
I brought table scraps, calling him by the secret name
I invented, he ran only to me. Above the grooved
rubber stairs of the hallway was a domed light,
always on, and I listened to the footsteps and voices
of the family upstairs, thinking about the family
of before, when my father was at home. "They lived
happily ever after," I read to myself under the light
as I finished each story I wrote with my bitten
pencil. But one morning, walking down into the new

stillness of the cellar, I discovered my cat was gone.
For days I called its name, searching the shadows
of the coal bin, and the space behind the furnace,
and the water tank with its cold, wet pipe, and the sills
of the cobwebbed windows. "When are you going
to come out of the clouds and join the world?"
my mother asked, shaking me. Then she sent me
outdoors to play with the upstairs children on the lawn,
which was where the confused man stumbled off
the sidewalk and went down on his knees
in front of me, asking me, among all the others,
to help him. I remember the handkerchief
he lifted from his weeping eye, and I recall
my sense of his fear as I bent close to his face
and he moved his pupil upward to show me the small,
retreating sliver which was the source of his pain
and weeping. I was unafraid, and I held his head
in my hand while I touched one corner of the cloth
on his open eye to remove the hurt, and when he stood
up at last and looked down at me, smiling, I felt
the happiness he felt, a child again, blinking and changed.

ON REWATCHING *SAMPSON AND DELILAH*

Down underneath, I could tell my mother
was as excited as anybody to be going to the drive-in
movie our minister recommended, which was why
she took so long preparing her picnic for the car
that she made us late. My stepfather got mad, as usual,
but I felt happy anyway because I was off my grounding
for the night and leaving behind my long day of work
on his goat farm. Crossing the river on the new bridge
into Ascutney, Vermont, seemed to me like a movie itself
as I sat at the window beside my two brothers,
looking up into its lit, shifting arches. The box office
that the arrow pointed to as we turned in
to the theater was an actual box, and I could see

from how my stepfather took the tickets from the man
in the window and called him "Bub," that he wasn't
so mad anymore. We found an empty space way
in the back row with a post next to it and a speaker
that clipped onto the window, which was my favorite
thing of all, because you could hear the voices
of the far-off people on the screen speaking to you right
inside your car in an almost secret way that had nothing
to do with their old-time expressions and bible costumes.
So when Delilah spoke to Samson after she kissed him,
it was clear to me she was sincere, just like
Carol Diamond was sincere when she kissed me
behind the school after junior choir on the night
I came home late and my stepfather got angry
and grounded me for the whole summer. It was hard
to watch Delilah, feeling the way she did, cut Samson's
hair entirely off so he no longer had the strength
to fight her people, the godless Philistines, and worse
to see the guards throw him in prison and blind him.
But it turned out, I was right. At the end of the movie
Delilah was true to Sampson, apologizing and leading him
between the two giant pillars of the temple courtyard
where the Philistines mocked him, so he could push
the pillars down on them. I punched my older brother
hard in the arm to show him how wrong he'd been
about Delilah all the times he elbowed me
about her cleavage. But he didn't punch me back,
because now, even he was caught up in how the base
of one pillar had actually started to move, slowly at first,
while the Philistines went quiet and everybody in our car
went quiet, gradually realizing as the pillars came down
and the false god with the belly of fire began to collapse,
that all the people in the courtyard would be buried,
including Samson and Delilah. It must have taken us
a long time to leave the theater after the screen
went blank and the cars lined up at the gate.
I don't recall, or remember how sad I must have been
as I sat thinking of blind Sampson turning away

from the awful thing God required of him, to call out
to Delilah for the last time. I don't even know
what Carol Diamond looked like on the worn copy
of her class picture that I kept in my cowboy wallet
and drew out to gaze at all that summer. But I still
remember, as we passed beyond the lights
of the Ascutney bridge on the way back to my new home,
the sudden rush of obligation I felt to the dream
of love I carried through the dark against the odds,
because that might have been the beginning of my life.

NIGHT RIDE IN WALMART

"The store takes away the keys at 11 p.m.," I tell the sad,
overweight woman limping toward the riding carts,
"but never mind, this is my dream cart." For a moment,
neither of us can quite believe how its fenders gleam

in the half-dark of the entryway, she touching its tufted
seat with wonder before she lifts her frayed coat
to slide in with her cane and adjust the rearview,
I settling in by her side. Then we're off through

the parting doors and past the disabled man who says
"Welcome to Walmart" with a special wave, because
he's sitting above a set of wheels, too. Who else
but she would know our first stop should be the wide

aisles of miraculous relief from distress and pain
and sleeplessness? Who else could cut such careful
arcs around the granny with pink hair just discovering
the island of first-time-ever discounts, and the slow

obese man, heading toward a forest of price rollback
smiley faces with a side-to-side walk resembling
her own sorrowful sashay? "Oh, bananas," she says
as we arrive in produce, meaning they're not regular

store bananas, browning before they turn yellow,
but perfect, dream bananas, which I jump out to gather
for our broad front basket, adding two exquisitely
aromatic melons for the basket in the rear. "Oh,

cabbages and cucumbers," she says, gliding to their place
in a green ocean of lettuce, spinach and peppers we have
all to ourselves. Only a dream cart could carry us
so quickly past the bald man at the mirror

in Men's Outerwear, who tries on a lone star hat
admiring himself as a Texas cowboy, and the two kids
who should be in bed but just want to be here,
yanking at the sleeves of their exhausted mother

among the vast shelves of new toys. For on this night
ride in Walmart, we, too, float on longing, no shelf
too high for us, though as the last announcement comes
over the intercom and the stockers begin their shift,

bringing more pallets of more for less down the main
aisle, the shelves seem to grow higher, and the aisle,
with its racks of DVD movies and boxes of floral
dinner settings and close-out microwaves, is so long

we can hardly see the disabled greeter with his back
to us at the front of the store, and the joyless line
of shoppers at the one lit cash register, and the doors
opening and closing on the heaven of appetite.

TOAST

Here's to the shock of the just then,
and the never saw it coming, the zig
when it should have zagged,

to the surprise of guess who,
guess what happened
and she did what,

and to the mortal embarrassment
of right in front of everybody,
and don't tell me my fly was open

all that time. Let's hear it for the foot
on the banana peel, the rug
pulled out from under us

and what we couldn't have imagined
would leave the whole thing
up in the air or up for grabs.

And here's to our prayers of thanks
for them, the holy shits,
no shits and are you shitting me's,

out of our mouths before we realize it,
grateful as we are to find
the words for the truth beyond

the same old, where life as we knew it
gives in by delight to all the shit
we don't know.

IN PRAISE OF A TREE

In the town photograph from 1905,
the white pine is already old. It lifts
its branches above the roof of our house.
Today, they are higher. When we tilt back our heads
to find where the tree has put its fine, feathery
crown, we can hardly avoid the sense of falling.
For two hundred years it has climbed

the ladder up out of itself, straight
and tall as its forbears, once chosen
to make masts for a king's warships.
Here in the grass by our front door, this tree,
which has done battle with wind and ice,
carrying cargoes of squirrels and songbirds
and flinging winged seeds to feed them
in spring, is a mother ship of its own making.
Forget that the great lower branch is broken,
and think of its struggle with the weight
of a two-day snow. And disregard the abandoned
woodpecker hole, now risen to the height
of our second floor. For on this May morning,
the morning of my poem, it became the home
of the honeybees. Think of them flying
across the sky to swarm the hole, while we,
in our excitement, threw open the storm
windows that had sealed us in. Imagine
the vibration of their single, omnipresent hum
as the tree took them into its ancient heart
singing this praise song, this music of the spheres.

THE MESSENGERS

The persistent yellow
of the dandelions, blooming
on the morning after

our mowing. The delicate,
torn gauze of cloud
that has never heard

of Constable clouds.
The heron beneath the heron
flying upside-down

in the pond's reflection,
and everything always
becoming what it's not

supposed to be: in spring,
the lost branch
by the stream

leafing slowly into a willow;
in fall, the milkweed pods
making the strangest beauty

from the lavender
on their hairy,
pimply skin, as if,

like the others,
they were calling us,
the supposers,

down from our lofty
presumptions of order,
though they just go on

changing, bringing
life as it is
right to our feet.

MAIYA'S GECKOS

Maiya likes having two geckos
in her room, she tells me
on the phone, because
they are like fancy plants.
"All you have to do, basically,"
she says, "is water them

and feed them in their tanks
once a day. Also, they change
colors, like when I feed the big one
banana mash, her stomach
turns yellow with brown spots,

and the little one, which I don't
dare to let out too much because
he's more feral, gets so excited
when I do that he turns this
dark black." It makes me,
her grandfather, laugh

to think of black as excitement,
and that makes her laugh, too,
though not out loud.
Maiya is the sort of person
who is serious and amused

at the same time, like when
she tells how her math teacher
teaches as if he's talking
to himself about what
he knows already, adding
that his mouth is always

a straight line so you can't see
what he's feeling and his head
is a square, which
for a math teacher
is ironic. She likes art class

but even there, is too shy
to raise her hand, she says,
disgusted with herself,
which should be my opportunity
to step in with some self-help.
But where does this talk

about the excitement of color
and the mockery of straight lines
lead, but to the possibility
of the art she creates each day
in her room with the geckos,

who don't even care she's there,
separate and strange and calm
as they are, until you release them.

THE LECTERN

When I remember the lectern
with its beautiful grain
on my high-school desk,

I do not think, as I did back then,
of my teachers in graduate school,
or my A-track students

bent over their desks in rows
taking notes, but of the boy
in C-track so determined to show

my lessons had nothing to do
with his life that he stopped
the class with his anger over

and over; or of the C-track girls
who wanted to know
my dog's name, and if

I was married, not incurious,
but curious in their own way;
or of the shop boy, Brad Butcher,

who made me the lectern,
asking his unexpected question
before he made it:

"Couldn't you sit down
on the edge of your desk,
like this, and just talk to us?"

AN APPRENTICE

Every day when we began,
I watched you in the mirror tying
a knot at your throat,
your face hopeful, your hands
tying the knot tighter, then turning

the pages of poems in a classroom
while you used a language
learned from others, longing
to speak the very language
you held in your hands.

It should have been easy for me,
your invisible companion,
the articulator and finder of forms,
to teach you then what seemed
so easy to me; yet you made

things difficult, returned to silence
by a thought you weren't prepared
to think, or by your insistence
on thinking through touch,
each word sensed

in a braille of images and feeling
as you searched for the truth
of what you were trying to say.

And when your first poems came at last,
it wasn't the lines you wrote

that excited you so much as breaking
them again and again to let in
the space around them, as if
you didn't trust the words I loved
without what wasn't words.

I admit I was slow to hear at the end
of your broken lines the cry
of an incomplete spirit
finding its way. And I confess
to my exasperation as I watched you

stop writing altogether to sit for months
in a circle of light while your close ones
lay in the dark above your head,
writing your lists of how, caught up
in your long, interior struggle,

you had failed them. For how else
but through your stumbling
and your tears could I have understood
the limits of my facility?
I was always incomplete

myself without your failures
and doubts, and your stubborn
allegiance to the heart.

NOPLACE

Where, looking down through the side window
of a monoplane, I found by surprise
no town, or road that could take you to it,
only a wilderness of forest.

Where, when we moved there,
the houses themselves seemed wild,
some with large butterflies on their clapboards,
or trees with plastic milk jugs bearing

colored water as a sign of welcome,
or actual signs, offering Egg's and Free Kitten's.
Where Denis Culley, told by his older neighbors
that his workhorse and friend, Dick,

was lonely without a mate, went
to the paddock in twilight after their work
together to stand quietly beside him.
Where our white terrier, Annie, escaped

to follow her nose down to the bog, returning
the next morning as a brown dog I didn't know
until I saw the mud. Where mud
was the name of a season, when the snow

that surrounded our houses suddenly melted,
leaving old Ralph True's yard so soft, he said
at the store, his truck went in, right up
to the tailpipe. Where springtime was the shock

of white blossoms on the pear trees
in our back yard, and every fall began
with Francis Fenton's poster of a single apple,
which meant all the different kinds

of Maine apples he harvested and sold
from the crates in his barn, saying their ancient
names in his high-pitched, jerky dialect
from a vanished time: Somerset, Thompson,

Kavanagh, Black Oxford, and the free one,
Dolly Delicious, preserving by its name and taste

267

his departed wife, Dolly Lee. Where winter, the longest
season, was dark and slow, like the plaintive voice

of Ethelyn Perkins, whose mother spoke in the same
slow way, as if they and the generations
who passed it down to them knew sorrow,
even in joy. Where beneath the play

of the wind in the all-night snowfalls that filled
our driveways and pathways while we slept, wrapping
snow high around our chimneys and bringing dunes
of it to our front doors, was the darkness

of its will to erase us. Where the bright room
of calm in the dark, for all seasons, was the hall
of the National Grange and Order
of the Patrons of Husbandry, where old farm tools

were fastened to the walls, and an American flag
hung beside the Maine state flag, with a farmer
and a moose that rested in the grass
beneath a perfect pine. Where the mural on the grand

drape was a lagoon in old Venice, a place where none
of the town elders had ever been, its strange,
painted gondolas equipped with sails, unknown
to gondolas before. Where the officers

wore blue sashes as they took their stations
and whispered the secret password to the Steward,
Francis Fenton, and his assistants, and they shared
words from another time and place

that lifted them up: *Let us be honest,*
be just, and fear not. Let us keep ourselves
unspotted from the world. Where, one by one,
they succumbed to the time-bound, spotted

world, Ralph and Dorothy True, Bob Hall,
Ruth and Clifford Tibbets, Ethel Herbert, Isadora
and Walter Tracy, Arnold Foss, and last,
Francis himself, with a three-gun military

salute at the church cemetery and the folding
of the stars and stripes, corner by corner,
in breathless silence, as for them all.
Where, but for our grief, it was a perfect day,

like the day when the plane turned high
in the air while I looked down for a town
that had disappeared into the vastness of forest
as if it was noplace at all, and I had only dreamed it.

WHERE I WOKE UP

After I fell, a man in a yellow coat leaned
so near my face he seemed to look
inside me for an answer, asking if I knew
where I was going, and in that pause,

while the vehicle that carried us turned,
then sped down a street, I, too,
listened inside myself. Was I lying
on the playground at school after
the swing knocked me out? The circle

of teachers' faces that looked down
as if through a hole in the top of my head,
became the faces of nurses in a hospital,
the nearest asking with an urgency

in her kind eyes where I was, then
when I was born, so I saw up close
the need to pay attention to where I was,

and who I was. Who was I?
In the night dark where I woke up,

what seemed at first to be a long shadow
between me and myself, the silent one
I'd listened for as I lay in the ambulance,
turned out to be a curtain

between me and someone in bed
on the other side. And when the nurses
swept the curtain back and guided me
through the doorway of the bathroom
turning on the light, a toilet,

mirror and towel bar jumped out at me
and I fell backward as if I were falling off
the ladder, as before, but now into the soft
hands and arms and breasts

of the nurses' embrace. Oh, I could have rested
with my eyes closed against the light,
free from falling, forever. But the next day,
hearing their warm voices saying Hon'
and Sweetie, I opened my eyes

to the light. Beyond the drawn curtain I saw
who it was they spoke to, an old,
exhausted man who seemed
exactly my age, his skin nearly

transparent against his white sheets,
and after they pressed the button to lift
me up in my bed, they lifted him, too,
holding him fast so he didn't slip
to one side where a stroke had undone him.

In the cafeteria, as a nurse helped me to a table
on my walker, I met others who had fallen—

off a motorcycle, on slick winter ice,
and by the quick surprise of a threshold

long taken for granted—all of us
assembled for breakfast and our daily
assignments, mine subtraction:
"When you carry what has been taken away,
then add up what you've lost, what

do you have left?" asked the therapist.
In my room, the last winter light vanishing
outside my window, a solemn man
with a briefcase, who once lay in this place

for weeks unable to speak, he said,
stood by my bed describing what happened
to him in a voice without tone or volume,
as from a distance he could never
close, though he shook my hand

and gave me a gray, photocopied
explanation of everything he thought then,
but could not say. All night the pain
in my head was my dream

of the terrible subtraction of saying. All night
when I woke, my eyes coming to know
the dark, a nurse held my head for a pill
or, not to stir my roommate as he slept,
whispered stories about her rescued cat,

as I, speaking as if for the first time,
whispered back. Oh, my healing began
with love, and with the sorrow
of lifting a walker over and over

down a long hall while my roommate
tried to sit up, falling back, and with the tears

of an old quilter in a wheelchair
who sat beside me after dinner, calling
to a nurse for the handcrafted bedspread

she kept in her room—the quilt, she said,
her husband liked best. She did not cry
because he lost himself piece by piece
before he died, but because of how the fine,

invisible stitching I felt with my hand
as she guided it over the beautiful
colors she'd spread across our laps
changed the quilt from pieces
into one whole thing. On the morning

I myself changed, a doctor in a white coat
looked down on me in my bed,
holding his clipboard to assess, he said,
my present situation. Then a small,

balding man in an ordinary sweatshirt
gave me a cane and walked with me,
assessing only the possibility of my hands
and feet. Did I know, he asked,
that Ben Hogan held a golf club as if

it were a baby bird trying to open
its wings? I felt the warm bird breathe
in my own hand as I loosened my grip
and walked step by step down the lit hall

of that hospital, until I reached the doorway
where he beckoned, walking backwards
in his excitement, and I found myself
standing before the practice stairs
of the gym. Oh, I opened my arms then,

touching the bars at each side to rise up
foot over foot, like flying. And in the moment
I turned to look back, I was both the one
who didn't know himself in the dark

and the others I had become. I was the surprised
balding man who now held my cane, smiling
up at me, and the helper who comforted
the old lady beside her on a bench. I was that lady,
and the man in a halo the nurse wheeled past

to bathe him, and the nurse, and my roommate
alone in his room, and the woman
who cried, guiding my hand over the fine,
mysterious stitching no one could see.

ACKNOWLEDGMENTS

Thanks to the following magazines in which my new poems, late wonders that came by surprise, originally appeared: *The American Journal of Poetry, Deep Water, Ibbetson Street Magazine,* and *The Innisfree Journal.* Special gratitude to the house of Godine for bringing into print nine of the ten volumes represented here, and to Joshua Bodwell, the best editor I have ever had, for his loving care with all aspects of this book.

A NOTE ABOUT THE AUTHOR

Wesley McNair is the author and editor of more than twenty books, including poetry, prose, and edited anthologies. His work has appeared in the Best American Poetry, more than sixty anthologies and textbooks, and been regularly featured on NPR.

McNair has held grants from the Fulbright and Guggenheim foundations, two Rockefeller grants for study at the Bellagio Center in Italy, two NEA fellowships, and a United States Artist Fellowship as one of America's "finest living artists." He has been awarded, amongst other prizes, the Robert Frost Prize, the Theodore Roethke Prize, the Jane Kenyon Award for Outstanding Book, an Emmy Award, the Sarah Josepha Hale Medal for distinguished contribution to the world of letters, and the PEN New England Award for Literary Excellence in Poetry.

McNair has twice been invited to read his poetry by the Library of Congress, and has served five times on the jury for the Pulitzer Prize in poetry. He served as Maine Poet Laureate from 2011 to 2016.

A teacher for several decades, McNair is currently professor emeritus and writer in residence at the University of Maine at Farmington.

A NOTE ON THE TYPE

Late Wonders has been set in Bembo, a design based on the types used by Italian Renaissance printer Aldus Manutius in his 1496 edition of Venetian poet Pietro Bembo's travelogue *de Aetna*. The typeface was a noticeable departure from the common pen-drawn calligraphy of the day. In 1929, Stanley Morison and the design staff of the English Monotype Corporation used punchcutter Francesco Griffo's original designs to create the type we know today as Bembo. McNair's first book published by Godine—1989's *The Town of No*—was also set in Bembo.

Design & Composition by Tammy Ackerman